¡Andamio!

Engaging Hispanic Families for ELL Success Using Brain-Based Learning

By

SUSAN F. TIERNO, Ed.D.

¡Andamio! Copyright© 2021 by Susan F. Tierno, Ed.D.

Andamio Press, LLC All rights reserved

ISBN: 978-0-578-85323-9

With the exception of short excerpts from articles, or other research material, no part of this work may be reproduced, transmitted, or stored in any form whatsoever, printed or electronic, without the prior written permission of the author and or publisher.

Cover Design: John Miller
Editing and Interior Design: Laura A. Marsala

First edition printed in 2019

DEDICATION

*To all the Mommies who understand
that education will open doors for their children.*

CONTENTS

Foreword
Dr. Ana Maria Rodriquez, "The National Opportunity for **Parent Engagement**: An Educator's Perspective"

Preface
Pat Campos, "Hispanic **Parent Engagement**: A Border City and State Perspective"

Introduction

Section I: Framing the Challenges
1. Defining the Issues
2. Developing a New Engagement **Model** for Hispanic Parents
3. Meeting Today's Challenges Head On

Section II: Constructing the Engagement Model
4. **Brain-Based** Learning - A Primer
5. The Basis for **Brain-Based** Parent Training Programs
6. **Brain** Basics
7. **Memory**
8. Food for Thought: The **Brain** and Food

Section III: Parent Training
9 Boots on the Ground: **Brain-Based** Training in Action
10 Parent Training
11 Parent Marketing 101: How to Fill a Room
12 Designing Welcoming Environments
13 Engagement Strategies
14 **Choreography**
15 A Fresh Approach: Structured **Mediate** Learning
16 **Brain-Based** Activities

Section IV: Measuring the Efficacy of Your Training Program
17 Evaluation
18 Training Feedback Tools
19 Conclusion

Afterword

Appendix
    Key Terms
    Coordinator Resources: Sample Surveys
    Sample Program RFP: Northeast U.S. School District
    Thought Leaders: Some Book Recommendations
    Acknowledgments
    Contributors
    Works Cited
    About the Author

¡ANDAMIO!

Andamio is the Spanish word for **scaffold**. As a noun, it is the perfect word to describe a framework, platform, or structure for creating **parent engagement**.

This book is a **scaffold**, written to describe and explain the requisites imperative for understanding how to structure, why you structure, what you structure, when you structure, and for whom you structure training to create real engagement for the Hispanic stakeholders in your community.

Once your **scaffold** is in place, you will be able to choreograph, organize, and plan around that meaningful nexus a community of stakeholders who come wanting and ready to learn.

In many ways, the brain is like the heart or lungs. Each organ has a natural function. The brain learns because that is its job. Moreover, the brain has a virtually inexhaustible capacity to learn. Each healthy human brain, irrespective of a person's age sex, nationality, or cultural background, comes equipped with a set of exceptional features...

— Caine & Caine

FOREWORD
The National Opportunity for Parent Engagement: An Educator's Perspective

By Dr. Ana Maria Rodriquez

For decades, educators have wrestled with issues related to the academic achievement of students. The role of **parent engagement** in the education of children has long been one of the challenges faced by school district administrators, support personnel, and teachers.

How to engage parents in the students' learning process can seem overwhelming to superintendents, administrators, and the parent coordinators who are charged with designing and implementing the programs. This issue also includes the teachers who interact with parents on an almost daily basis.

This national opportunity for **parent engagement** encompasses a growing population of Hispanic parents, whose children's first language is not English, adding another layer of complexity.

Fortunately, we now have a book that contains a balance of thought leadership and pragmatic guidance for administrators, parent coordinators, and teachers facing that complexity.

Uniquely qualified, Susan F. Tierno, Ed.D., provides leadership and guidance in this arena. Her decades of experience, her research, her "boots on the ground" approach, and her specific knowledge of 21st-century educational barriers for Hispanic families serve as the foundation for this "why and how to" book.

Not only does she recommend processes and procedures based on her knowledge, experience, and research, but the solutions she offers are based on recent, repeated successes in actual implementation of the ideas with Hispanic parents.

Grounded in the concepts of community building, equity, **brain-based** learning, and social emotional learning, this book represents a major step forward in how we can approach and influence **parent engagement** in our schools.

It contributes to the literature about factors in why some Hispanic children succeed in learning and others struggle to learn. I suggest that engagement of Hispanic parents in the education of their children is a significant factor: *¡Andamio!* provides a **scaffold** for educators to make that engagement happen.

PREFACE
Hispanic Parent Engagement: A Border City and State Perspective

By Pat Campos, Title I Parent and Family Engagement Coordinator, Laredo Independent School District, Laredo, Texas

I have been working with families for 30 years, much of that within the juvenile justice system. I am currently a Title I Coordinator in a Texas border city and serve on a statewide **parent engagement** council.

We have 28 Title I campuses in our district covering pre-K to Grade 12. I have 28 parent liaisons and a lead staff person to help me fulfill my mission.

Parent engagement was not happening previously. How do I know this? Throughout the juvenile justice system we saw the results when were parents not involved with their children and their studies.

It's not that the parents don't care. They just may not know how to ask for help. They may not always understand our education "lingo."

In response, we took our nighttime ESL classes and offered them as day classes for parents who were not working. Other parents told us, "I have three jobs and I'm trying to make ends meet. I don't have time to make it to the parent trainings."

We began teaching them skills that they could turn into part-time income, such as classes on making paper flowers, edible arrangements, wreaths, cake decorating. We taught them how to use the computer and social media to promote their fledgling enterprises. They all have phones, so we taught them how to use the phone apps that would help them sell their products.

The extra income allowed many of those parents to drop one of their multiple jobs and attend our trainings. Instead of 40 to 50 parents participating monthly, we now have 180 to 200 **engaged** parents. Plus, they're excited about what they're learning.

Because our **parent engagement** program has been a successful **model** program, I was invited to serve on the Texas Council for Family/School Engagement by our statewide Title I Coordinator. I also spent a week at Harvard University to learn more about **parent engagement** from national thought leaders on the topic.

I believe that ¡Andamio! is significant and relevant because parents want to know how to help their children throughout their educational journey. Parent trainings are essential in order for true engagement to take place.

I can tell you that Susan's **model** works. I personally observed how much it helped the parents from our district who participated in this training.

As a **Parent Engagement** Coordinator, I would ask teachers and school administrators to consider the following five questions:

1. Do you know the parents by name?
2. Do you know the family dynamics?
3. Do you know if they have a job?
4. Do you know if they care about school?
5. Do you know what they want from school for their children?

If you can know your parents by name and to this personal level, then you are well on the way to success.

One hundred years from now it will not matter what my bank account was, the sort of house I lived in, or the kind of car I drove, but ... the world MAY be different because I was important in the life of a child.

— Author unknown

INTRODUCTION

Throughout my life, education in its many forms has been my passion and purpose. Like my siblings, friends, and colleagues, I have spent many years contemplating and pondering over the marvels of the learning process, especially for children. I knew at a very young age that I would somehow use my deep love of learning and teaching. I knew that my life was going to be about a motive and purpose far greater than myself. Helping children to learn emerged as my motive; to assist them on the wonderful journey of learning emerged as my passion and purpose.

The book you are holding in your hands is not only the story and testimony of my work, but also a real and tested research **model** or tool for **stakeholder** guidance in our **communities**. It is my intentional and purposeful effort to help our diverse school **communities**.

In 2016, I brought the field of English Language Learners (ELL) **parent engagement** one step forward with my doctoral dissertation, *"An Exploration of the Impact of **Brain-Based** Training on Hispanic Parents of English Language Learner*

Elementary-Age Children." My dissertation chairperson encouraged me to bring forward my legacy of engaging Hispanic parents through **brain-based** training over the course of 15 years.

As a community builder, education advocate, teacher, and social entrepreneur, I could not stop there. This book represents an extension of my dissertation research, a distillation of the current research, and key concepts. It is a pragmatic guide and template to show you how to build a **parent engagement** program that works. Build it right, and "they will come".

WHO WILL BENEFIT FROM THIS BOOK?

This book is multifaceted and designed with several audiences in mind:

To **school superintendents and administrators:** Here is a breakthrough solution to your myriad challenges. The most dynamic elements of my extensive "boots on the ground" research and implementation in school districts in five states were the extended length the program was allowed to continue and fidelity to the program's process and concepts. There is no question that, over the course of 15 years, the **model** produced similar positive results throughout, as evidenced by federal and private evaluators.

The book is not a technical, academic book. It is a template for creating **parent engagement** through **brain-based** learning initiatives. It uses several approaches that draw parents into **engagement**, specifically, in Hispanic districts and schools. It is the roadmap and execution document for your Title I programs.

To **Title I Coordinators**: This book is your template for forming, launching, and sustaining a thriving **Parent and Family Engagement** Department.

In these pages you will find both the why and the how for successful capacity-building **model** with **strategies** that optimize teacher, ELL parent, and ELL student engagement. I have designed this book to include best practices in diverse environments based on my experience and research. In the back of the book, I have included an effective **model** grant that has proved its worth.

To **teachers**: Here is your support, your introduction to quelling fears about parents in the community. As you follow my precepts, questions, and guidance, I hope you find that your students will engage their parents, and you will reach out and develop a strong **relationship** with each one of the parents from your classroom.

MAKING A BRAIN-BASED CONNECTION

Over the years, I have studied much about the **brain** and its machinations. The study of the **brain** as it relates to thinking and learning is one of my established axioms in what I do for children, parents, and teachers. In short, it is one of my most important principles, something to which I adhere as I teach, talk, develop, or publish. The **brain** is the core. What follows are a few distilled ideas we share with parents in my engagement **model**.

The human **brain** is a unique phenomenon purposefully gelled together in some marvelous achievement of creation and nature. Weighing a mere three pounds and containing more than 100 billion cells, the **brain** constantly performs a sophisticated orchestration of purpose and flexibility.

It is unlike any computer designed. Advances in neuroscience continually reveal new capacity, capabilities, and adaptabilities with direct implications for educational goals and initiatives. As a teacher and trainer, I cannot conceive of fostering **parental engagement** or student learning without serious understanding of the **brain**'s parts, functions, and contribution.

The following **nine words** are extremely important to **parent engagement** and **brain-based learning** in this book. I highlight them for you here, at the beginning, so you will recognize them as you read further and they will reinforce my concepts. Think of them as signposts or indications that you are on the right path.

Brain	Brain-Based	Choreography
Communities	Engaged	Mediating
Memory	Model	Parent Engagement
Scaffold		

I am extremely grateful for my own Think and Learn Coaches (TLCs), or project teachers, as well as colleagues and collaborators who contributed immensely to the development and guidance of this work over time, which has now become ¡Andamio!.

I am especially thankful to all the parents over the years who trained under this **model**, but most recently to the 40 Hispanic mothers in a southern Texas border town, who participated in the major phenomenological research around the training and reminded me of a parent's own potential. After all, a parent is a child's first teacher.

I am happy to share my vision and experiences with you, and it is my hope you will incorporate them successfully into your daily work as a formative, informative, transformative, and reformative tool.

Susan F. Tierno, Ed.D.

Section I
Framing the Challenges

CHAPTER 1
Defining the Issues

A healthy community is a thick system of relationships. It is irregular, dynamic, organic, and personal. Neighbors show up to help out when your workload is heavy, and you show up when theirs is. In a rich community, people are up in one another's business, know each other's secrets, walk with each other in times of grief, and celebrate together in times of joy. In a rich community, people help raise one another's kids. In these kinds of communities, which were typical in all human history until the last sixty years, or so, people extended to neighbors the sorts of devotion that today we extend only to family. Neighbors needed one another to flourish and survive--to harvest crops, to share in hard times.

— David Brooks, **The Second Mountain**

COMMUNITIES

As an Army brat and a teacher, I have lived in many different **communities** over the years. It is very clear that the **communities** of the past are not quite the same as today's

communities. However, when I compare them all, only one thing comes to mind: We live in **communities**.

So, what are **communities**? An encompassing definition for a **community** found in a second grade social studies book describes it as, "a place where people work, live and play together."

As an ecosystem, **communities** encompass myriad schools with visions and missions, each containing all manner of stakeholders. A most essential **stakeholder** group comprises **parents** of children growing up within the **community**.

> *What we have in common helps us form our sense of community.*
>
> — Marx, 2014

¡Andamio! is somewhat of a memoir, initiated by what was uncovered and discovered through my research with Hispanic parents of ELL children in grades pre-K to four in a community on the southern border of Texas.

I designed, developed, and implemented my **model** as a process for bilingual programs in large city schools in order to form purposeful relationships with bilingual teachers and Hispanic parents through **brain-based** learning in school **communities**.

Community, capacity, relationship building (also called social capital building), thinking skills, and empowering parents as leaders are at the core of what I determined to be the most transformative parts of my process **model** to help ELL students succeed in school and help their parents in become **engaged**.

Not all Hispanic adults have attended school in the American education system. Because of this, what parents want for their children and what they would like to see in our schools varies from what they themselves experienced in school even 15 to 20 years ago.

Our **communities** and schools, however, are rapidly changing. They are dynamic in nature, evolving culturally, educationally, and technologically.

Efforts to build social capital, or dynamic relationships, in the Hispanic **communities** are well documented in research and were intended to improve the reading or math skills of neighborhood children. Hispanic women, we found, specifically enjoyed forming relationships with other parents and developing networks of friends through the community-building process during training and beyond.

CHANGING DEMOGRAPHICS

Over the last 30 years, large metropolitan areas, such as Los Angeles, New York, and Chicago, and states—including Arizona, Florida, and Texas—have seen a significant influx of English language learners. In the 1990s, this language demographic shift moved up the I-5, I-35, and I-95 corridors to include Georgia, South and North Carolina, Virginia, Rhode Island, and Massachusetts. Driven largely by employment trends and opportunities, this shift affected schools and impacted **communities**.

Currently, nearly every school district in the country—including so-called "flyover states" such as Nebraska, Iowa, and Minnesota—is being impacted by very diverse and multilingual language groups and related social issues that include poverty, high mobility, instability, and equity.

According to the 2010 Census, the young and fast-growing school-aged Hispanic and ELL population numbered more than 13 million. According to the 2020 enrollment data in K-

12 schools, Hispanic students now comprise anywhere from 22.7 to 25% of all students in kindergarten through Grade 12 classrooms, and that number is expected to continue to grow.

For example, Rice University researcher Steve Murdock estimated that by 2040, Hispanics will make up 62% of population growth in the United States, producing upward of 40% of the school-aged children nationwide. The significance of the Hispanic demographic shift affects how American public schools will serve ELL students in the best way. This shift has a direct impact on how we establish relationships with their **communities** and families to ensure success for all children in our schools. Most specifically, with the trend of online, distance learning for K-12, the challenge is to address the critical question head on: How can we design our 21st-century curricula to address this shifting demographic and cultural transformations?

Of the 3.7 million K-12 teachers across America as of 2010, less than 1% of public school teachers are ESL instructors. That means that there is just one ESL instructor for every 150 ESL students compared to the standard classroom ratio of one teacher to every 15 students. Of those teachers who serve ELLs, fewer than 8% have bilingual-ESL certifications. There are not nearly enough teachers to service the ELL school population now, much less as we move into the future.

To compound the lack of trained ESL instructors, 38% of the American workforce comprises millennials (adults between the ages of 22 and 38 years old in 2019). These young people have used computers, laptops, phones, and other electronic devices since they began school, and their usage levels are comfortable. Many of them were hired as teachers in our school **communities**. However, many millennial teachers have not worked with diverse populations, especially children of poverty.

The shift in the age and experience of today's teachers matters because very little current professional development for teachers and parents includes wholistic approaches to address equity, poverty, diversity, changes in national standards, changes caused by the need for distance learning, and testing in our classrooms. The majority of younger teachers have learned to teach to a test instead of being trained to understand how children think and learn.

> *The brain processes information all the time. It digests experience to some extent in the same way that we digest food. It is always responding to the complex global context in which it is immersed. Educators must come to grips with that fact. Brain-based education involves experiences and meaning.*
>
> — Caine & Caine

THE IMPACT OF TECHNOLOGY

> *Technology is a great tool, but it is only one modality. Proficiency requires our students to be masters of many modalities, including old-fashioned print and face-to-face exchange.*
>
> — Louise El Yaafouri

To further compound the challenges that teachers face with changing demographics, they are also teaching children who are now referred to by some as the *Swipe Generation* because of the impact 21st-century technology has had on them. In other words, the younger generation's **brain**s have adapted their neurotransmitters to process information in a completely different way than those of generations older than millennials. Because of these different processes, it is often challenging for teachers and parents to know how to engage students with curiosity, interest, and investment.

The *Swipe Generation* refers to children who grew up after Apple's Steve Jobs introduced the first iPhone in 2007, phones one could swipe to get something, go somewhere, and gain information fast. Concurrent with the release of the iPhone, Jeff Bezos at Amazon released Kindle, an electronic book format that was read by swiping the pages.

Hispanic parents in particular flocked to these new electronic devices to enhance communication with their families and stay informed about school, child, and home, thus becoming digital immigrants. Meanwhile, their children were introduced to and immersed in the new technology at various stages in school as they learned new skills for the first time, making them digital natives at a very early age. The trend toward distance and online teaching has rendered the use of electronic devices essential for learning, from pre-K on up. Therefore, the parent cellphone plays a vital role in the child's ability to complete schoolwork online and stay connected to the school community.

According to Pew Research, the vast majority of Americans (96%) now own a cellphone. Cellphone ownership now encompasses every demographic group.

The current generation of Hispanic parents is completely occupied, absorbed, consumed, and, in a growing number of cases, obsessed with their tablets, iPads, smartphones, and the accompanying myriad social media held on these electronic devices.

> *Physical and social technologies have now evolved....We have no choice but to learn to adapt to this new pace of change.*
>
> — Thomas Friedman

Designed to be used intuitively, today's devices are so easy to learn that even our youngest children can navigate them. However, overuse by children is the concern of many, if not all, the Hispanic mothers, for many reasons, including long online hours leading to **brain** fatigue, not enough devices for all the children in a household, outdated software and devices and the prohibitive cost to replace them. Many Hispanic mothers do not have experience using iPads and computers.

> *We are the first generation of parents that has to do this monitoring....Can you tell me what device I can use to fix the problem ... what it is I need to understand about the devices and how to control the habit my kids have formed with their device ...*
>
> — Kamenetz & Weiner

Rapidly changing technology has catapulted us into unprecedented social change and awareness, leaving us unprepared but accountable, to address the consequences of this social and emotional upheaval.

Not only do we have instant access to information 24/7, our digital behavior has now become embedded into our nervous systems and those of our parents and their children.

MONITORING AND MEDIATING ONLINE LEARNING

> *[Digital] Games provide a narrative world of meaning, consequence, and relevance to motivate and engage players. The core question of learning games is one of transfer.*
>
> — Justin Reich

Today's children love games, just as they always have. The history of games goes back thousands of years. Board and dice games go back almost 5,000 years. Today's games are different, but they still play an integral role in learning and socialization. Playing games creates the ability to focus and imagine scenarios. Games stress the ability to make choices. Most significantly, games help children develop the ability to follow directions and rules, build meaning and consequences, and transfer the skills via games that they are learning—all critical skills.

Digital games have changed education via online learning. However, while computer games appeal to human intuition, they don't instruct children as to how to stay on the task at hand. Furthermore, Justin Reich noted that while those who play the "working **memory**" digital games with vigor do get better at other digital games, they do not necessarily improve in cognitive tasks. When playing digital games, children often can't make the decisions that are best for them if left unattended for long periods of time. Without mediation, it is easy for them to become distracted by the images and options the programs include. Therefore, mediation and monitoring by adults becomes necessary to ensure that the games are being used for the intended purpose. The teacher or parent still has a real role to play in online learning.

Today's ELL children love to compete in games on electronic tablets and computers. They compete for points. The faster the game goes, the louder and more **engaged** the students become, sometimes culminating in an argument or disruptive behavior.

Mediating and media mentoring from a parent perspective can help our ELL children to look at the emotional effects of competition and help them observe the difference between competition and cooperation. That fast-paced competition with its accompanying aggressive behavior has become a toxin in the **brains** of our children. The more parents leave their children alone using a tablet or smartphone, participating in social media, or playing a computer game, the moodier the children become. Parents want to know how to manage and control this new issue.

SO WHAT DO WE DO?

The new phenomenon of learning online via cell phones, computers and pads — in the classroom, and at home — has demonstrated that our youngest generation has **brain** changes that allow them to learn in milliseconds. Students learn differently from those of past generations and require more help with their thinking, socio-emotional learning, and **memory** in many ways. Are today's parents equipped to handle these physiological changes in their child's **brain**? Do they know the best ways to use this information in order to help their children learn?

According to David Eagleman, a child's **brain** needs to be activated through engagement via social interactivity. The **brain**'s neural plasticity needs to change. Parents and teachers need to explain and have clear activities that require the full engagement of both learner and teacher, investment in helping the child to learn, and a curiosity in how to accomplish this.

A new practice, termed media mentoring, has emerged in both technology education and socio-emotional learning and now serves as a guideline offered by the American Academy of Pediatrics.

> *Mentoring means understanding the media that kids use.*
>
> — Kamenetz & Weiner

Specifically, media mentoring (or **mediating**) is contrary to what parents and teachers are currently doing, which is scheduling, managing, and controlling our children's time on electronic devices.

Mentoring is a form of **mediated learning** wherein a parent, as a learning coach, observes to see the emotional effect the technology—devices, software, and games—has on the children who use it. Herein, it becomes a process of both decision-making and socio-emotional learning strategies for parents with their own children to help them understand what is real and what is simulated.

Currently, not only is access to both physical and social technology expected for school learning, but also, our children are delving into the deep dark Internet during school, after school, and throughout the night when they should be sleeping.

Both teachers and parents need to learn the strategies for **mediated** learning, mentoring, and monitoring children in their behaviors when using technology.

Educators are introducing students to a variety of engaging educational learning apps and devices for reading and math. The children, however, often come to school already having the savvy and tech skills needed to explore and learn. Schools need to focus on professional development for teachers and parents on how to **mediate** and mentor for quality socio-emotional growth, but they also need to focus on parental controls and locks for the children's protection.

On the other hand, the new technology (particularly smartphones) has its advantages in **communities**, especially with Hispanic parents, who are, according to research, more inclined to network socially. This is a great advantage with scheduling, communicating, community building, or working on reading or math with their children at home. By utilizing apps in daily communications (such as Dojos and

Remind), parents can track their children's behavior and stay informed immediately of any issue that comes up regarding their children's activities and learning.

Technology has touched everyone in some way and changed the **brain**s, the nervous systems, and, most significantly, the moods of our children. Now, the work begins.

> *Fortunately, new technology tools will aid this endeavor ... at a minimum, our educational systems must be retooled to maximize these needed skills and attributes: strong fundamentals in writing, reading, coding and math; creativity, critical thinking, communication and collaboration—at every level.*
>
> — Thomas Friedman

CHAPTER 2
Developing a New Engagement Model for Parents

Families not only learn how they can increase their children's learning and become partners at the school, they also participate in school leadership ... They become the family ambassadors at the school, reaching out to other families and engaging them in sessions that increase their knowledge and presents an opportunity for them to be engaged at the school.

— Maria S. Quezada, Ph.D.

In developing a new **engagement model** for parents, there needs to be a completely new way of thinking, planning, relating, and implementing. The **model** needs to be nontraditional and, significantly, more relational than what has been presented at workshops in the past.

Due to an emphasis on increasing parent involvement in past years, schools turned to hosting traditional events that were expected to increase parent attendance at school-related functions. Some of the functions have been one- or two-hour events such as open houses, back-to-school nights, parent-teacher conferences, celebrations, student performances, multicultural festivals, parent information sessions, and workshops on various topics.

Although these traditional efforts of school sponsored-events might be useful, they are not aimed at purposefully improving student behavior or accelerating student learning. These types of events merely inform and involve parents with information regarding their child in school, such as immunizations, parent-teacher conferences, and school operating procedures.

> *While family involvement activities have been required in federally-funded and most state-funded educational programs since the 1960s, it is still the least understood or implemented of the key elements of educational reform.*
>
> — Maria S. Quezada

At the midrange of **parent engagement** activities that have a slightly higher level of impact on student learning are parent training institutes and academies, back-to-school nights, and interactive homework, especially for distance and online learning. Like any other school-driven practice or initiative, well-planned, -designed and -implemented events that are actively supported and valued by stakeholders in the school community have greater potential for success.

In developing my **model**, I found that by helping parents become aware of their child's learning behaviors through **brain-based** learning in school, at home they are more inclined to put greater emphasis on their children completing homework and on the importance of their studies. My research indicates that these initiatives have greater impact on student academic growth.

What can we do to better prepare parents for connection to their children's learning at school and home in a landscape of rapidly changing technology?

THREE COMMUNITY-BUILDING PILLARS
Pillar #1: Involved vs. Engaged Parents

Changing demographics show an increased diversity that is predominately Hispanic in our public schools. For the most part, ineffective, inequitable school systems often cause Hispanic parents to become disenfranchised, even in predominantly Hispanic school districts.

The goal of my **model** is to illustrate how to increase the number of parents who participate in training and **engage** them in several areas of knowledge, including child and age development, **brain** growth, language development, reading and literacy, as well as food and other environmental factors that affect child development and the thinking and learning process in the **brain**.

The above goal is a very different stepping stone as opposed to merely involving parents who attend some random back-to-school informational event.

Engaged parents are empowered and motivated, and take a more active role in their child's thinking and learning, because they personally learn the how (or process) of learning and the why (or reasons to learn) in order to help their children at home more effectively.

Truly **engaged** parents are not just checking the box with attendance at parent meetings and going home more overwhelmed and confused than when they arrived. **Engaged** parents begin to build relationships with each other, with the school, and with the community.

Research on building relationships with families shows that the relationships nurtured and developed with the families in the school community are of the utmost significance. Fostering these relationships for our communities of color, however, means honoring what they bring to school.

— Maria S. Quezada, Ph.D.

Engaged parents ask questions, give feedback at trainings, and contribute more to the decision-making process that has a direct impact on the success or failure of their children. **Engaged** parents, captivated by listening to new information and what that information may mean for their children, are full of questions.

As one parent in the training noted, "I learned from all the days (of training) to be patient ... that no matter what the problem is there is a way to teach and learn, so that our kids can come forward on their own." **Engaged** parents are absorbed by taking notes, hungry for take-home materials, eager to translate this learning to the home. One parent stated, "Three steps for directions is less harsh on my children and helps them to pay attention more."

Engaged parents are no longer on the sidelines "just trying to help," one parent noted. **Engaged** parents become more informed. Informed and resourceful parents understand the role of the **brain** in their children's learning process and are advocates for integrating as many forms of cognitive support in the way of strategies as possible. These are **engaged** parents.

My research strongly suggests that parents of ELLs need well-defined training that connects and bridges the strategies for learning from school to home in a sustainable way by learning about the **brain**. Through active engagement, parents train in processes and procedures that signal better **memory, connections, and thinking in the brain.**

Pillar #2: Learning to Learn Parent Engagement

Parents are a child's first teachers. Parents can help their children to learn. Pattern repetition and developing dialogues with a child are critical at a very early age. When children learn how to learn from an adult, they become better listeners and develop more critical learning behaviors in a classroom at school. **Parent engagement** can lead to greater improvement in student learning behaviors.

> *When a task is roughly aligned with our larger goals, our brain circuitry comes to reflect it.*
>
> — David Eagleman

Before effective **parent engagement** training can be developed, several questions need to be explored in order to understand the specific needs of the group. The following is a guideline that will help establish what is important to them and determine if they are aware of their children's needs.

1. Does your child listen? Can your child repeat what you have just stated?
2. Does your child understand the directions you give?
3. Does your child understand boundaries?
4. Does your child want to learn to read? Does your child know why reading is important?
5. Does your child like math?
6. What interests your child?

Several questions need exploration by administrators:

1. Do you know the parents by name?
2. Do you know their family dynamics?
3. Do you know why they are living in the school neighborhood?
4. Do you know who their friends and neighbors are?
5. Do you know if they trust anyone?
6. Do you know if they have a job?
7. Do you know who watches their children?
8. Do you know if they care about school? If so, what do they want from school for their children?
9. Do they monitor how late their children stay up at night?
10. Do they feed their children on a fixed schedule?

Posing both sets of questions in the planning stages may reveal insightful information. For our parents, the ongoing preoccupation with "How is my child doing in school?" has already been measured by myriad standardized state exams, but those test scores do not reveal the learning barriers that their face.

My experiences have informed me that parents want to know the strategies for thinking, along with how to make it happen. There are, however, greater possibilities for parents who are **engaged** with the school in order to help their children work toward academic success.

In my **model** of **parent engagement**, ELL students and their parents learn to think on their own and become self-directed learners. Hispanic parents are taught about the **brain**, about what, why, and how **brains** connect to think and about how to think about what they are learning. Simply stated, this is called metacognition.

New **brain** cells form every time a child has a new idea, thought, or experience. Stressing this to parents is critical because they tend to do everything for their children. When ELL students and their parents acquire new learning about the **brain**, they become much more resourceful about reaching academic and family goals. My research shows they learn how to become much more curious, creating a desire and motivation to read and write on a regular basis, which is essential for their future.

Pillar #3: Teacher Engagement

When more inclusive, *equitable* learning environments prosper, it leads to more meaningful and productive classrooms. In its early iteration, my **model** invited the parents to come into classrooms after full training to work on strategies with their children.

When parents come to school consistently and communicate quickly as it relates to their child, teachers are more able to help students learn how to synthesize, evaluate, and create with the information they are learning in the classroom. The one thing that is very difficult to change in the classroom is the home stress.

> *Chronic and acute stress is hardwired into children's developing brains ... Compared with a healthy neuron, a stressed neuron generates a weaker signal, handles less blood flow, processes less oxygen, and extends fewer connective branches to nearby cells....Unpredictable stressors severely impair the brain's capacity to learn and remember.*
>
> — Eric Jensen

Parents want and need to become aware of what is happening both at home and in the classroom in order to support what their children are learning at school. So too, it helps learning how to become **engaged** in supporting their children in the learning process at home. As a result, parents are more prepared to understand and address questions such as the following:

1. How is my child listening? What are the ways to listen?
2. How do the interruptions in the classroom affect my child?
3. What kind of learning issues affect my child?
4. What does my child need to understand about the directions for homework?
5. How does the food in the cafeteria affect my child?

OPTIMAL SCHOOLS

Optimal literally means power and resources *(ops-)* applied to the very best *(-tumos)* in order to create a new state. In biology, optimal refers to "conditions most favorable" to support life.

As the term *optimal* relates to this book, it is about building **communities** of informed and **engaged** parents in geographical areas that are traditionally — or have become — disenfranchised. Though economically poor, these **communities** are socially and culturally rich and able to reach optimal levels that lead to engagement.

My training **model** is about what schools can do to support parents in the thinking and learning process of children, even to the extent of understanding the meaning of standardized testing. When the focus is on the students' experience in education, the process of **parent engagement** transforms, creating a ripple effect that will ultimately benefit teachers, administrators, and the greater community. A mirrored **model** is built around a sole focus or goal. All schools and districts can create a **model** built around a nexus with their own content. My mirrored **model** of engagement and the **brain** produces thinkers and learners.

THINK & LEARN PARENT ENGAGEMENT MODEL

My **mirrored model** (see figure below) is designed for parents whose children and their teachers participate in **brain-based** training.

Think & Learn
An Integrated Model for True Parent Partnerships!

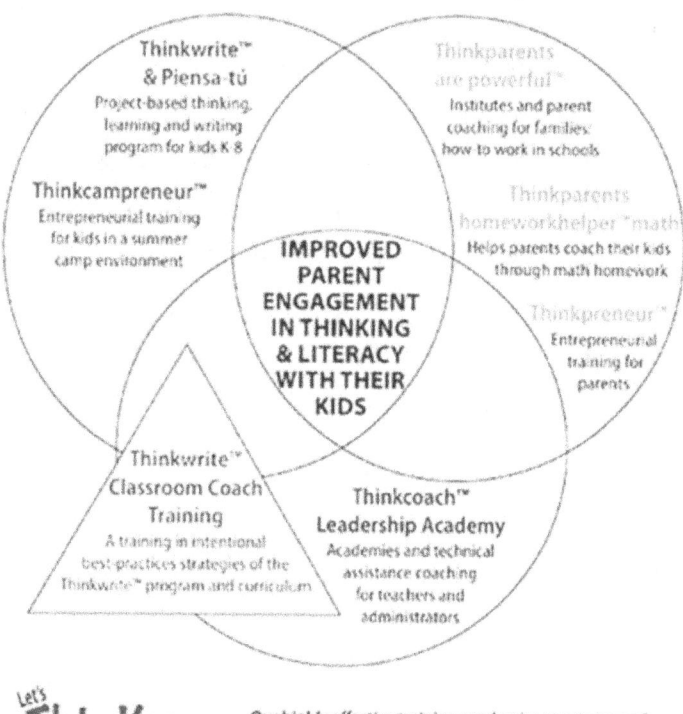

Highly structured, the **parent engagement model** called *Think & Learn* was created based on extensive research and first-hand experience in school districts in five states over the course of a decade. The **model** represents the best practices from **brain-based** research, as well as the programs for teachers, parents, and students. The research included direct feedback from parents who participated in all **brain-based** training sessions.

The **model**, with its intentional **brain-based** habits, is not only about the school-to-home relationship between teacher and parent. It is about developing intentional strategies within activities that helped parents and teachers become **engaged** and stay **engaged**. This happens by focusing on purpose, social responsibility, and social and emotional support of family. So, too, the **model** and its training hones parent skills to align with cognitive development, thinking and learning, as well as socio-emotional development for both parent and child.

CHAPTER 3
Meeting Today's Challenges Head On

In many poor households, parental education is substandard, time is short, and warm emotions are at a premium---all factors that put the attunement process at risk. Caregivers tend to be overworked, overstressed, and authoritarian with children, using the same harsh disciplinary strategies used by their own parents. They often lack warmth and sensitivity and fail to form solid, healthy relationships with their children.

— Eric Jensen

In each school district used for my **brain-based** training research, including inner city and suburban environments, and one of the fastest-growing border cities in Texas, a short survey was given to Hispanic parents. In the most recent research, 40 parents took a preliminary survey. I looked for their relationship, beliefs, interests, background, and their own education histories as part of the orientation for the **brain-based** training.

Like Hispanic parents in the large city school districts, many parents who took the most recent survey remembered learning basic academic subjects in school. They rarely recalled getting off task, emotional challenges, health and safety issues, or social challenges as it related to how their children were learning at school or at home. They also realized that life in the world of fast-paced changes included the new reality of online and distance learning and technological changes.

STRESS LEVELS

One area that parents considered to be of significant concern was the level of stress that they were observing in their children as it related to school and testing. Added to this, parents noted a number of additional stressful situations, such as homework, new math, and reading for meaning.

Some parents expressed concern that in addition to issues at home, the schools were becoming harmful to their children's health.

> *Common issues in low-income families include depression, chemical dependence, and hectic work schedules—all factors that interfere with the healthy attachments that foster children's self-esteem, sense of mastery of their environment, and optimistic attitudes.*
>
> — Eric Jensen

Consequently, what the parents wanted for their children was less stress at school, more reading, and more of an understanding about the academic work their children were required to complete, including homework.

Most parents expressed difficulty and frustration in knowing how to assist their children with homework. "I try to help him so he knows what he has to do," said one participant. "I look for someone older, like an older child, or someone who speaks

English, who can explain the directions to an assignment, so I can help."

Parents who wanted to become more involved in their child's school expressed disappointment that teachers did not allow parents to come into the classrooms and did not answer emails requesting assistance concerning what their child needed to complete their homework.

My research showed repeatedly that, in general, teachers were not very helpful to parents. Parents need the relationship with teachers to be more of a partnership, one that is sustained over time, a relationship that is easy to reach, advise, and inform.

Parents responded overwhelmingly that they usually sat with and helped their children as much as possible, as indicated by the most frequent responses: "I sit with them," "I sit down with them; I try to explain to them," and "I help them."

21ST-CENTURY BARRIERS

My research exposed the following 21st-century barriers for parents when it involves their children, school, and home. The results were the following: **Cognitive impact, socio-emotional impact,** and **social capital-building impact**.

Cognitive Impact

Parents Unaware of the Role of the Brain and Learning

> Often, poor children live in chaotic, unstable households. They are more likely to come from single guardian homes, and their parents or caregivers are less emotionally responsive.... Young children are especially vulnerable to the negative effects of change, disruption, and uncertainty. Developing children need reliable caregivers

who offer high predictability, or their brains will typically develop adverse adaptive responses. Chronic socioeconomic deprivation can create environments that undermine the development of self and the capacity for self-determination and self-efficacy.

— Eric Jensen

The results of my research indicated that parents know very little about the **brain**. Nor do they know how it works in developing learning behaviors and thinking processes.

By initiating and raising parental awareness of the role of the **brain** in the home and then the learning process, parents are more likely to consider taking advantage of the myriad cognitive influences and training at their disposal. Most notably, when parents understand more about elements needed for an optimal student learning experience, they become more interested in being a more "relevant" role **model** for their children and stronger advocates for student learning.

Emotional Impact

Barriers have social and emotional impact on parents that is reflected in their approach to their children and their school, their role as a parent, and their purpose to their families.

Emotional barriers are often difficult to manage on a day-to-day basis because common issues—such as depression, chemical dependence, or feeding children on a timely, routine schedule—become too much for parents of ELL children. These factors lead to unhappy and often unhealthy attachments. Behavioral issues and poor school performance lead to poor academics.

From my experiences, there is one key point about our ELLs that I have learned. Many times, ELL children stay at the homes of their grandparents after school. They watch novelas all night long and see the behaviors of adults talking appallingly to each other on these TV shows. Then they come to school and emulate that behavior and language with other children. Mothers need to intervene once this behavior is explained.

Social Capital Building

When we hold conversations about **communities** of poverty and their schools, we attempt to talk about disturbing stressors that are interfering and intrusive issues.

The phrase *social capital* suggests measuring stressors in numbers. This is common practice in school districts. My research, however, demonstrated that Hispanic families and the parent participants involved in the trainings were a bit different, building on purposeful relationships.

> A social community is healthy when relationships are felt deeply, when there are histories of trust, a shared sense of mutual belonging, norms of mutual commitment, habits of mutual assistance, and real affection from one heart and soul to another.
>
> — David Brooks

Social capital building refers to training parents in the organization of their time and family time. Parents noted this concept required patience in learning how to organize.

Social capital building became critical to communication with their families. Listening, organizing, and using words such as *partnership, roles, planning,* and *communication* were highly favored after several days of training.

Limited Resources and Time

Programs organized and directed by schools do not always acknowledge or appreciate parent schedules and other demands on their time. Some areas of concern include parent meetings scheduled at times inconvenient for the parents.

Parents are often working two jobs. Childcare services need to be available for younger children of the family. Most significantly, when possible, meals, sandwiches, or light refreshments are important to include because hunger is often a real issue or they may have skipped a meal in order to make time to attend the meeting.

Language and Culture

Prior to the 21st century, language and cultural barriers primarily focused on language, in terms of Spanish or English. Today, the focus is on "What is my child supposed to be learning?" and "What do the directions say for the child to do in order to complete the homework?" When teachers do not relay or explain this information clearly, it causes barriers between parents and school.

DETERMINING THE NEEDS OF A DIVERSE GROUP

Often, **parent engagement** coordinators ask me for suggestions or tips on what the program for diverse parents should look like based on the diversity of the school.

When reflecting on this question, my first thought is that everything should encompass a **nexus**, or focal point. In order to stay focused, the coordinators will need to bring together the members of the community with all of the stakeholders circling around one positional point. For example, on our team, we call our **nexus** "improving **parent engagement** in thinking and literacy with their kids."

It starts with the **brain**. In my axiom, the **brain** comes first because God made the **brain**. The **brain** is the only thing that formulates a human differentiation from every other animal that is living on Earth.

I encourage **parent engagement** coordinators to think of **models** to use. Key to selecting and implementing a **model** are surveys that are distributed to parents and stakeholders. Surveys include questions about the issues with which they are dealing and issues they would like to have covered in a training. Here are some examples:

- What do they already know?
- What do they need to know?
- What do they want to know?

Determine the central **nexus** first. Coordinators need to decide the central **nexus** based on parent and stakeholder input.

Coordinators need to define and understand the demographics of the city and what populations the schools serve. This will dictate what **model** to select.

Diversity is the customer that you are going to serve. The product is the training, the new thoughts, and your information, as well as the formation and reformation that they will walk away with.

Language and Training Environment

Another variation of the **parent engagement** coordinator question involves the wide variety of languages spoken by parents, such as Somali, Burmese, Swahili, or Arabic. Program coordinators will want to know how impactful the training would be if they translate and interpret the training for the parents.

Language is important, but training environment is important as well. More emphasis should be placed on what grade levels and ages work best together. For example, mommies with same-aged children work better together.

If you are looking to translate, I would recommend spending some of your Title I money to invest in translation devices. We use them in several school districts with great success and the come with a menu of hundreds of languages.

I recently transferred from a school district—the 18th largest in the country—that uses a tool called *Language Links*. Anybody in any district school, any administrator or teacher, can pick up the telephone and be connected instantly with a continuously monitored call center. The school administrator might state, "I have a mother here who only speaks Mandarin. Can you help me?" On the other end of the line, a language translator from some far-off location will come on the phone and begin speaking Mandarin (or whatever language is needed) to help translate. *Language Links* is probably one of the best **models** for administrators to facilitate communication with our diverse populations of parents.

Information and Expectations

Gaps occur between an assignment given in the classroom and the discussion of the assignment at the dining room table. For example, children forget what to do, or how to do the homework. Think about the implications from the classic "Telephone Game," where a simple phrase within a small circle of individuals starts with one person, who whispers the phrase to the next person in line. In turn, that person whispers the phrase to the next person in line and so on. By the time the last person receives the phrase and states it out loud, it has morphed into something very different from the original phrase. This is what happens to homework assignments.

Are the instructions that were given during the school day going to be understood when the student and parent finally sit down to discuss an assignment later in the evening?

Challenging Home Environments

Engaged parents try to view the home environment as a learning center as opposed to a hectic space with television at the center. Job schedules can cause chaos, and activities are often unsupervised. Parents begin to realize that economics plays a big role. They need to assess influences that are detrimental to their children completing assignments by providing needed resources and structured support, making sure that they eat healthy meals and go to bed at a reasonable hour.

What do ELL parents need to know to be efficient, effective, and **engaged** helpers at home for their child at school? Through research, I discovered that several elements were often missing in the home that would facilitate parents in helping their children. The elements were:

- A space of their own for homework or distance learning
- Structure in routine
- Consistency in meals and habits
- An organized environment

Any one of the individual barriers to a community could prove detrimental to engaging parents in order to help their ELL children with school success. My research showed that not only do multiple barriers exist, but also that there is often low awareness of the barriers among parents and school personnel. A full-force commitment must come from the district to address these barriers, and it starts effectively with **brain-based** learning.

Section II
Constructing the Engagement Model

CHAPTER 4
Brain-Based Learning: A Primary

The new paradigm for achieving excellence through equity is grounded in knowledge derived from three important areas of research: (1) child development, (2) neuroscience, and (3) environmental influences on child development and learning.

— Blankstein & Noguera

Brain-based learning refers to teaching and learning approaches, methods, and intentional strategies that use myriad styles and types of activities — especially as they relate to cognitive development — and how students learn differently as they age, grow, and mature socially, emotionally, and cognitively.

Brain-based learning, first noted by Leslie Hart in the 1970s as **brain**-compatible learning, is driven by the general idea that learning can be improved and more efficient if educators base how and what they teach on the neuroscience of thinking and learning. What parts of the **brain** connect to make learning more efficient and productive, as well as long lasting, in the **brain's memory**? This question shifts the emphasis from past educational practices of following the latest teacher's standards, or established conventions, to knowledge about how to think and how to learn. Intelligence for all children then is the ability to learn and understand any information.

For example, it was commonly believed that intelligence was a fixed characteristic that remained largely unchanged throughout a person's life. However, recent discoveries in cognitive science have revealed that the human **brain** physically changes when it learns, and that after practicing certain skills, it becomes increasingly easier to continue learning and improve those skills.

The findings that learning effectively improves **brain** functioning, resiliency, and working intelligence has potentially far-reaching implications for how schools can design their academic programs and how teachers could structure educational experiences in the classroom.

In the mid 1990s, I began assembling a mirrored **model** of training for Hispanic parents. I analyzed the works of many researchers and authors. Some of the authors were already researching and writing about the **brain** and learning. One researcher was Leslie Hart, who started the movement advocating the **brain's** role in learning, well before educators accepted the idea. In *The Human* **Brain** *and Human Learning* (1983), Hart describes the **brain's** patterns and programs as representing both understandings and skills. Hart emphasized the importance of feedback for correcting and strengthening **brain** functions and the vital aspect of acceptance and support of the learner in contrast to fear and harm.

In the 1990s, Rennate and Gregory Caine produced a profound and innovative book, *Making Connections*, on the

brain and **brain-based** learning. Explaining how the **brain** works to think, connect, and learn, Caine and Caine discuss active questioning, pattern building, creativity, using a variety of memories, the ability to self-correct and self-reflect, problem-solving, processing information to increase meaning and comprehension, among other concepts. Almost 30 years later, we are slowly seeing these changes in strategic approaches to learning both in classrooms and for adult training.

Educational leader and former teacher Eric Jensen continues to write about and affect our thinking on the **brain** and learning. His most recent book, *Teaching with Poverty in Mind*, discusses the fundamentals of key topics or themes needed for parents in poverty who want to learn more about active and **engaged** training. Below are 10 of his concepts that I have generalized for you.

1. Mental **Model**s: What previous ideas or notions do you have?
2. Movement and Learning: Tactile and kinesthetic movement such as dance and play.
3. Emotional States: How you feel when you are happy, sad, worried.
4. Physical Environment: A place to sit, write, act, move, and play.
5. The Social **Brain**: How we learn to talk and act with one another.
6. Motivation and Engagement: When an adult is included in one of the above.
7. Critical Thinking Skills: Questioning, inferring, receiving, perceiving, organizing.
8. **Memory** and Recall: Fun, quick games to build the **memory** patterns.

9. Teacher-Trainer Influence: Sharing how the trainer thinks, perceives, and forms ideas.
10. School and District Environments: How to act in different environments; how to build relationships and keep them.

Educational consultant David Sousa, who writes about the **brain** and learning, is another favorite author of mine. In his work, he discusses how **brain-based** research reveals what happens during the process of language development.

This happens to be a key theme about which many parents are interested in learning more. Specifically, they want age-appropriate development tips. Because of this interest, we stress in our training **model** the following about learning and the **brain** — as opposed to screaming one- or two-word commands at their children:

> *The brain acquires, stores, and recognizes words. But to communicate effectively, the words must be arranged in a sequence that makes sense. Languages have developed rules that govern the order of words so that speakers of the language can understand each other.*
>
> — David Sousa

Parents come to training sessions with preconceptions. It is, therefore, important for them to gain an initial understanding about the **brain** and language development.

Brain themes need to relate to one another in some pattern or unique way, such as **scaffold**ing. Parents need factual knowledge and the context of activities in order to understand new information and organize the facts and information in a conceptual framework so that the information they share with their children will make sense.

For parents, **scaffold**ing and organizing information has to be simplistic enough to retrieve the information from their **memory** in order to apply it sometime in the near future. **Memory** forms through sound, symbols, numbers, and patterns that include such processes in both the right and left **brain**.

BRAIN B.I.T.S.™
Bilingual Integrated Thematic Strategies

The following five tables from my research outline the various stages of the **brain**'s development. This information was analyzed and formed into a mini-book about the **brain** called **Brain** b.i.t.s™ for use in training of my parents. I find these chunks of information are helpful as a simple way to illustrate the key stages of **brain** and social development, from birth to age 17. Activities and questions formed around these tables encourage parents to answer and dialogue within their teams.

Here are a few of the questions posed to the parents as they consider their children through each stage:

1. What age is your child now?
2. What do you think about your child's growth?
3. What have you observed in terms of play, speech, emotions, and movement?
4. How many of you have older children?
5. Do they act like the description for their age?
6. What age and growth step do you think they are exhibiting?
7. What are some concerns you have with your younger children?
8. What might your concerns be with the older children?

We ask the parents to discuss their answers, ideas, thoughts, opinions, and beliefs in teams. We found this exercise to be highly beneficial for parents.

Stages of brain development
Birth to age 4

Brain Bits	Socio-emotional Bits
• Organizes information before birth.	• Models one to one.
• Develops birth to 2 years, cell structure for movement.	• Counts 1, 2, 3.
	• Has strong preferences.
• Sensory areas begin to mature.	• Matches sounds and letters.
• Forms auditory 'maps' by age 1 and words by age 2.	• Imagines, uses fantasy.
	• Engages in cooperative play.
• Increases **brain** patterns listening to music.	• Builds patterns.
	• Cuts on line with scissors.
• Builds motor development perceptual skills.	• Dresses self.
	• Makes designs.

Stages of brain development
Age 5 to 7

Brain Bits

- Has longer attention span.
- Has capacity to change focus of attention.
- Develops use of past and present.
- Does more **thinking** in deciding and judging.
- Complete control of fingertips.
- Complete sensory-motor system.

Socio-emotional Bits

- Shares and participates in organized games.
- Expresses feelings freely.
- Develops delayed gratification.
- Skips, hops, walks straight.
- Fold paper.
- Copies designs, letters, numbers.

Stages of brain development
Age 8 to 10

Brain Bits	Socio-emotional Bits
• Develops lengthy attention span. • Develops greater perception of time. • Understands cause and effect. • Reasons logical to practical. • Develops planning as a skill.	• Works in small co-operative groups. • Accepts responsibility. • Understands rules. • Sets standards. • Competes. • Is sensitive. • Understands cause and effect. • Understands concepts of time.

Stages of brain development
Age 11 to 13

Brain Bits

- Develops thinking about thinking.
- Emotional limbic system is wired.
- A period of brain growth occurs.
- Critical thinking and reasoning develops.
- Can solve problems systematically.
- Improved motor development and coordination.
- Practice in decision making.
- Able to deal with abstraction.

Socio-emotional Bits

- Impact of peers important.
- Achieves role.
- Has self-understanding and identity.
- Team-member.
- Self-cognition.
- Developing socially-responsible behavior.
- Little to some awareness of career or training for job abilities.
- Concepts of time.
- Developing knowledge and skills for society and civic awareness and role.
- Formal thinking related to performance.

Stages of brain development
Age 14 to 17

Brain Bits	Socio-emotional Bits
• A plateau of brain growth begins. • Need to refine the control systems of the brain. • Pre-frontal lobes growth: longest of brain's development process.	• Needs challenge of complex and abstract reasoning tasks. • Need for positive social relationships with peers. • Physical growth spurts bring on concerns over appearances and abilities. • Wants independence and needs love. • Needs structure and clear boundaries.

CHAPTER 5
The Basis for Brain-Based Parent Training Programs

In many ways, the brain is like the heart or lungs. Each organ has a natural function. The brain learns because that is its job. Moreover, the brain has a virtually inexhaustible capacity to learn. Each healthy human brain, irrespective of a person's age, sex, nationality, or cultural background, comes equipped with a set of exceptional features: the ability to detect patterns and make approximations, a phenomenal capacity for various types of memory, the ability to self-correct and learn from experience...and an inexhaustible capacity to create.

— Caine & Caine

Since 1995, I developed, directed, and implemented research projects that served more than 1,800 Hispanic, African-American, and other diverse immigrant parents (mostly mothers) in five urban centers.

In 2015, I replicated the **model** I had developed with a phenomenological (qualitative) research study of 40 Hispanic parents. The research validated and added to my work and the emerging research.

My study brought **brain-based** research forward into the 21st century with three groups (Hispanic parents, their children, and their children's teachers), so that it is up to date and will withstand the scrutiny of school district and state administrators.

I found that there are three basic needs in designing and implementing **brain-based** parent training:

1. Developing relationships with the parents (of ELLs)
2. Providing structured parent training
3. Building capacity as participants and coaches

I learned that developing relationships with parents of ELLs in a community was only the first of three steps needed in a process used for development and implementation of parent trainings. In the first step of the relationship, parents become aware of what their child's **brain** or cognitive needs are at each age level when they go to school **(low-level need)**.

In the second step, structured parent training takes place, which equips parents with knowledge about the **brain**, its functions, its capacity to learn skills, hands-on engaging activities with **model**ing, and intentional strategies in order to learn skills **(mid-level need)**.

In the third step, true empowerment and **engaged** learning for capacity building takes place. In this stage, parents are better prepared to enter classrooms equipped with specific strategies to assist with the learning process **(higher-level need)**.

This is also the level at which the parents are able to work with and train other parents within their community **(coaching and capacity-building level)**.

Designed to help parents coach their children to think, the **brain-based parent engagement** approach—based largely on following a process—aids parents in reading, writing, and learning more effectively. Knowing the three levels of need helps parents of ELLs to participate and engage fully in their child's education.

The **model** program develops parents' competencies (knowledge, skills, and attitudes) in the strategies and coaching skills to help their children become better questioners and critical thinkers. Further, it helps parents leverage their efforts with homework and classroom projects, questioning strategies, and strategies that bridge school learning to home learning.

Brain-based training is a structured, hands-on, constructivist, fully **engaged**, experience-based format in which parents of ELLs learn the principles of thinking and learning and the meaning of intelligence.

> *Intelligence is sometimes described as a patchwork of know-how and know-what areas in the brain, all those perceptual mechanisms so sensitive to expectations.... Intelligence is about the process of improvising and polishing on the time scale of thought and action. Intelligence is the ability to learn, exercise judgment, and be imaginative.... It is the capacity for thinking abstractly for reasoning and for organizing large quantities of information into meaningful systems.*
> — William H. Calvin

THE CONSTRUCTS OF TRAINING

Training requires quite a bit of thinking on my part. The theory of *constructivism* is the foundation for the training **model**, and is heavily embedded in **model**ing and demonstrating how the **brain** thinks and learns.

Constructivism refers to how learners actively construct or make new knowledge based on their knowledge and understanding of their prior experiences. In training, this constructive process enhances the capacity of stakeholders to cooperate, collaborate, and form teams in order to create a new learning experience together, based on their collective prior knowledge and experiences. The formation of patterns during this interaction blends preceding knowledge and new information that impacts learning and comprehension. A parent training system creates, builds, organizes, and analyzes how to internalize the new facts and information.]

> *In a team, adults build relationships. In the relationship, parents become aware of what their child's cognitive needs are when they go to school. Parents learn how to follow process and procedure so as to keep focus on the information being shared.*
>
> — Susan F. Tierno

Constructivism can be compared to **scaffold**ing, or a step-by-step building of concepts and ideas, to build human thinking and learning. The **scaffold** provides the simple structure needed to construct ideas into more complex learning. Simply stated, first present an idea or concept. Next, present information and facts. Form teams to apply and explore the ideas, one step building on another.

Three principles are formed during the training **scaffold**:

- Concepts
- Constructs
- **Scaffold**s

These three principles should be included in every training.

CHAPTER 6
Brain Basics

The human brain is the most complicated object in the known universe. A single brain contains more electrical connections than there are galaxies in space. Understanding the behavior of its eighty-six billion neurons is as formidable a scientific challenge as interstellar travel.

— Raffi Khatchadourian, The New Yorker

Each part of the **brain** has a responsibility for a specific type of learning. Presenting the parts of the **brain**, and what those parts do, helps Hispanic parents understand home behavior, learning, auditory, visual, and emotional development.

Every talk, dialogue, and discussion in a parent training should help parents learn how their children think. Give parents a list of concepts and activities to build their knowledge. In my training programs, we play games with two sets of Word Sort concept cards, which are color-coded. In the blue set, each card contains a theme that is ultimately used to select research projects. In the pink set, each card contains a **brain** strategy word. Both these sets of cards are useful for sorting, ABC ordering, creating sentences, and grouping, which are all essential to creating and ordering language.

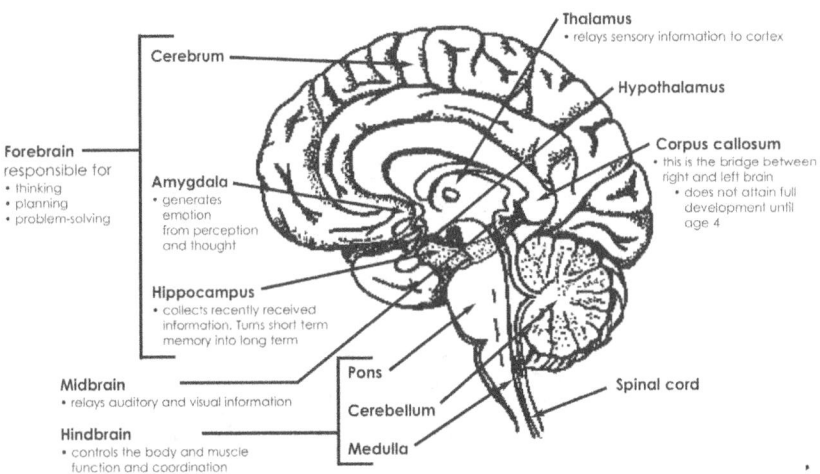

Brain: The **brain** is the thinking center. The **brain** is used for connecting you to clues, facts, and ideas. The **brain** takes clues, facts, and ideas and then connects them to begin to form thinking.

Clues, facts, and ideas: Clues, facts, and ideas are bits of information stored in dendrites. Gathering and using information can help you to learn many ways to think more efficiently.

Connections: Connections are clues, facts, and ideas that assemble and **scaffold** together to form thinking into patterns.

Dendrite: A dendrite is a road-like structure of nerve cells in the **brain**. There a billions of them in the **brain**. They are connecting all the time. A dendrite connects the thinking action to other dendrites. The dendrite connections create thinking systems.

The brain connects structures for **thinking**. These structures are called **dendrites**.

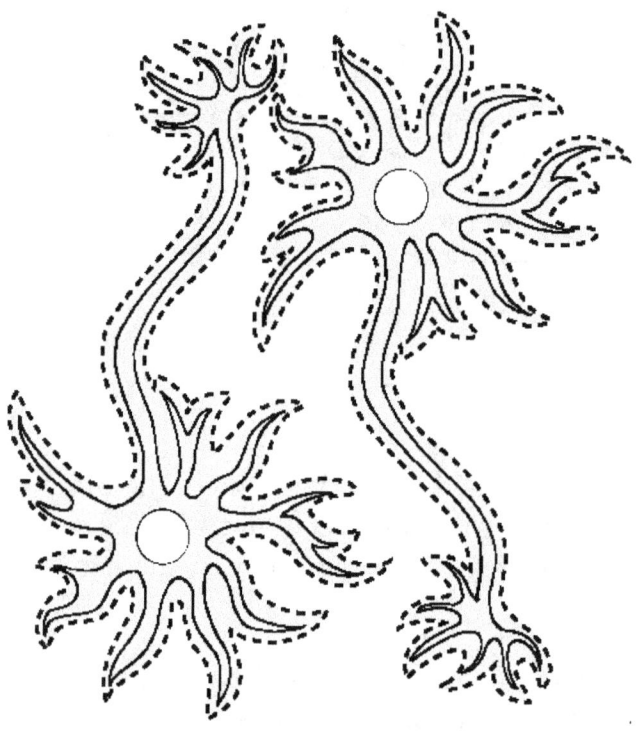

Learning: Learning is connecting your thinking strategies to discover and form new ideas.

Left Brain: The left side of the **brain** is the part that helps you to work step-by-step. It helps you to develop a plan and organize logically. The left **brain** also deals with numbers and symbols.

Patterns: Patterns are repeated connection of clues, facts, and ideas that organize into thinking patterns. The **brain** has systems for connecting the clues, facts, and ideas called thinking patterns.

Process: Process comprises the steps used in **scaffold**ing thinking. First, next, and last is a process.

Right Brain: The right side of the **brain** creates a picture and connects patterns and thinking through feelings, music, art, and dance.

Thinking: Thinking happens when a dendrite connects to another dendrite in a search to find and form new thoughts and ideas.

In the course of my parent training, one of the most critical things that I share is the substance, size, nature, and essence of what the **brain** looks and feels like, and how much the **brain** weighs. We share **brain** parts in games; we pass around rubber **brains** to hold and feel that are almost the exact weight of a real **brain**.

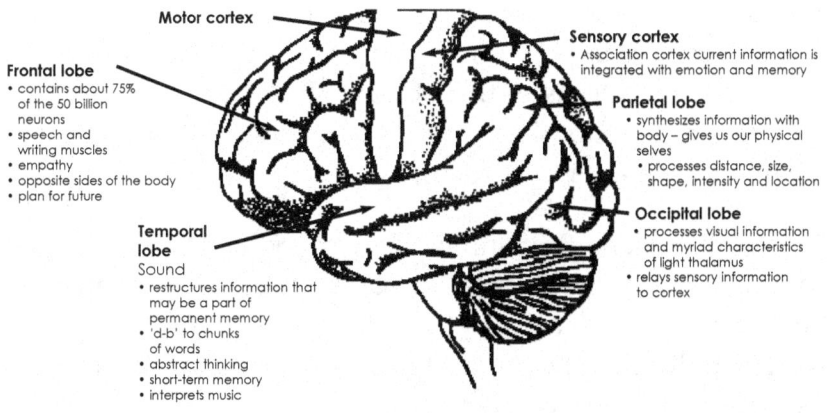

I like to have **models** of **brains** on the table. I like to have everyone wear **brain** hats. I have the parents color, cut out, and paste puzzle pieces of the **brain**. I designed a set of puzzle pieces for use in a kinesthetic game. Everybody gets a puzzle piece and runs to around the room to find the part that fits with the other parts of the **brain**.

By doing this, kinesthetically, we want to help parents understand that there are parts of the **brain** they need to know in order to help their children become more efficient in what they do. By the end of the game, a new team emerges, each with its fully formed puzzle of the **brain**.

The **brain** stores information. Once we begin to do a search of that information, the thinking connections begin. The **brain** also stores information on structures and functions in our day-to-day life. It provides the information on patterns for learning. There is a part of the **brain** for everything we do.

One **brain-based** strategy I use for teacher and parent training is Word Sort. Similar to the pink and blue concept cards, Word Sort helps parents learn about words with patterns, such as **-ee** and **-ea** (in words such as treat, feet, beat, or street), which are essential for the **brain** to capture language. Words with these patterns are hard for ELL students. They continuously misspell the words because they have not captured the patterns in their **brains**. If the parents are away of these concepts, they are able to help their children recognize the patterns in reading.

Once they see a pattern and work with the pattern repeatedly using colors, symbols, cut-and-paste activities, and puzzles, the **brain** automatically begins to provide information to them in patterns. They learn to spell words more efficiently, and thus use them more effectively.

In sharing the Word Sort strategy with parents, it is important that they understand that each part of the **brain** has responsibilities for thinking, and each part of the **brain** has responsibilities for learning. Complete connections cause children to think much more efficiently and productively with words.

I like to take the time to talk about how the **brain** connects structures for thinking. We even form a Circle of Knowledge (COK) and build a web of connecting dendrites in a big circle.

I talk about the dendrites and their neurons. The neurons carry information, and the dendrites connect to other pieces, folders, and compartments in the **brain** that store information.

An example of connecting dendrites is having parents help their children who have no understanding of an important element in a story. Parents don't understand connectivity so, through an activity, I encourage them to read a story to their children and then ask them questions such as, "What is the meaning?", "How is it like something you do?", "When or where have you heard about that before?". In this way, parents are helping their children recognize and connect the important elements. Parents need to know how to help their children connect those particular structures of thinking in order to form lasting comprehension.

I also remind the parents that safety, social issues, environmental, and technology issues affect thinking and learning connections. This adverse assortment of factors, more than anything else today, is a paramount theme for our parents to learn and discuss in teams.

CHAPTER 7
Memory

We tend to think of memories as snapshots from family albums that, if stored properly, could be retrieved in precisely the same condition in which they were put away. But we now know that we do not record our experiences the way a camera records them. Our memories work differently. We extract key elements from our experiences and store them. We then recreate or reconstruct our experiences rather than retrieve copies of them. Sometimes in the process of reconstructing we add on feelings, beliefs or even knowledge we obtained after the experience...

— Daniel Schacter

The **brain** stores critical pieces of information, forming **memory**. **Memory** is one of the **brain**'s great and mysterious functions. It is indispensable to all human beings. **Memory** is the connection in the **brain** that gives a human — from birth to old age — the ability to survive, endure, and persevere.

Although nothing is stored in the **memory** loop, **memory** is at the core of learning. **Memory** is sorted into categories. Despite this new age of massive information, **memory** is still not infallible. **Memory** causes many thinking and learning problems. The **memory** loop is the most important part of the **brain** because children need to connect and hold a *sense of memory.*

Helping parents to understand **memory** and its failure to function supports them in understanding **brain** strategies that will help with the malfunction of **memory**.

I find **memory** interesting because I did not think my second graders were listening to me enough. I have the same rules, the same procedures that I have probably repeated 100 times over 100 days.

Toward the end of the school year, some of the students in my own classroom whom I thought were never listening to my direction, were able to say to their peers, "She said, 'Sit down and be real quiet.'"; "She said, 'Put your pencil on your desk.'"; "She said, 'Take the pencil out of your hand because you can't listen if your hands are moving.'" It was amazing to me that they stored those pieces, those rules and procedures so that their **brains** could operate more efficiently.

In order to teach my parents about the concept of **memory**, I made a random, 90-second recording from a radio station in Mexico. We then shared it with the Hispanic parents in the group. You can imagine what 90 seconds sounded like: a staccato, rapid-fire cacophony of Spanish that started and stopped ever so suddenly, so much so, that it was almost incomprehensible.

The parents listened to the clip. They laughed hysterically. We stopped sharing the clip. I asked them, "What does this make you think of?"

During the discussion about the clip, the parents noted that the tone and the message did not match. The point was that the more they talk to their children, the less the children are listening. I elaborated for deeper understanding:

"Let me connect for you what this is like in terms of dealing with your children's **brains**. Your children's **brains** only hear a quarter, or less, of what you are saying to them. The less you say in trying to explain something, the better it is for them. Give one command, two commands, but no more than three commands. Don't explain why. Your children's **brains** operate just like this radio. I call this **Radio Brain**."

They laughed hysterically because they recognized their part in it. As a parent, you keep talking away, and although they know you are speaking, your children are not concentrating or focusing on you or the message you are trying to convey.

> *I try to show why memory is a mainly reliable guide to our pasts and futures, though it sometimes lets us down in annoying but revealing ways.*
>
> — Daniel Schacter

Parents always want to know, "When my kids' **brains** change, will their behavior change if I do these things that you're recommending for them?"

Plasticity (the products and materials in the **brain**) can grow dramatically and change over time. I explain to the parents that our children only think in small, quick jumps due to exposure to modern technology (Remember the *Swipe Generation*?). I tell them, "The more you help your children with **memory** and patterns, and the less extraneous information that's said, the better focused your child can be in their thinking." There is a point of intersection between attention and **memory**. Three steps, short directions, and eye contact helps to build better focus.

Memory is all about emotion. Most people do not realize that. It is at the core of our training. The **brain** connects with the emotional "self" in the amygdala portion of the **brain**, the limbic system of the **brain**. Our emotions affect our **brains**.

When a child is upset or trying to remember something, it interrupts the process going on in the **memory** loop. I can see it in children. It is classic conditioning.

I ask them to sit still for a second, or say, "You're moving too much," or, "You're trying to finish my sentences. Just listen. Just use your ears this time. Use your ears and your eyes to take in information. Do not say anything because that affects somebody else's **memory**."

> *The memory should be specially taxed in our youth, in youth, since it is then that it is strongest and most tenacious. So things you teach children at the earliest of ages, is the best because children are remembering. But in choosing the things that should be committed to memory, the utmost care and forethought must be exercised as lessons.*
>
> — Daniel Schacter

A researcher recently shared that most childhood traumas (big "T" for traumas and little "t" for traumas that accumulate), occur between the ages of 4 and 12 in a child's life. The **memory** stores the thought, the emotion, and experience into systems of **memory**.

The **memory** contains folders. Throughout life we **scaffold** the folders recreating those traumas on myriad scales via our **memory**.

Faces change and events change, but children respond the same as they did when they were the age the real trauma occurred. When we try to understand parents, we must remember that reactive emotion is likely from a childhood trauma. This is one reason we use a Make-a-Plan strategy during the training: to keep everyone calm and organized. It helps to keep all directions in three steps.

I've taught all my students the three steps (First, Next, Last) of the Make-a-Plan strategy. "Your first step says this, your second step says this. Your last step says this. It is color-coded for you." By the end of the year, my children were using their color-coded plans.

"Here is the First step. What does it say you have to do? Here is the Next step. What does it say to do in the Last step? Did you write your sentences? What part of the plan did you read or did you not read?"

Scaffolds and steps are about making **memory** retainable and usable. **Memory** allows us a past and a record of the past for who we were and who we are in human individuality.

If you did not have **memory**, life would be a series of meaningless encounters that had no link. My cat has a **memory**. She knows exactly where I am standing in the kitchen to ask for a treat. A dog has memories. He knows exactly how it feels when somebody touches him. Their memories are about predictable patterns, but are embedded in their emotions. I am very sure we can learn something from the dog and the cat.

Our **memories**, however, are larger, more concentrated, and more technical in our own **brain** than that of a cat or dog. I share with the parents that for all practical purposes, the **brain** stores an unlimited amount of information with approximately 100 billion neurons, thousands of dendrites, and the potential neuropathways that are incomprehensible.

I explain to parents about the 50 to 100 billion neurons in the frontal lobe. I also tell them that these myriad neurons help us with speech, language, sight, and thinking as well as muscle movements. They also help us with how meaningful the connections are as the inner workings of the **brain**. The **memory** cells store and plan for the future.

Part of the future is reading. Reading is about getting children to the neural pathway of emotion and the significance of emotion in a story. In reading Kate DiCamillo's books, such as *Because of Winn Dixie* or *The Miraculous Journey of Edward Tulane*, I may read a short passage and explain that those words mean love. Those words mean she loves her friends. Those words from the witch mean you have to love in life because if you don't love in life, what will that leave for you? For ELL students, this process of explanation is very significant because it helps them to associate emotion with words, actions, and reactions.

> *The definitive explanation for memory is still very elusive. Nevertheless, neuroscientists have discovered numerous mechanisms that occur in the brain, that, taken together define a workable hypothesis about memory formation (encoding), storage and recall.*
>
> — David Sousa

I discovered through my research that **memory** is what is most important for parents, Hispanic parents. How do you break the idea down? How do you store it in your cells in the **brain**? How do you then recall it again?

One effective way to help children recall things is by using colored sticky pads and highlighters; it is the color code for their Word Sorts and easily used at home. For example, students and parents using colors remembered all the **-ly** words because the **-ly** words were always blue sorts.

I advise Hispanic parents not to do everything for their children, especially their boys. Many want to do everything for their children: dress them, help them eat, or feed them their breakfast. It is important, however, to reinforce just the opposite. I share with parents that the **brain** literally develops, changes, and creates new cells each time it learns a new task.

I tell all parents, "Allow your children to learn a task and build **brain** cells. Do not do everything for them." Every time I see a grandfather or father come to school and take the backpack off the child's shoulder and carry it for them, I say to the child, "I'm sorry. Your backpack is your responsibility. You know how to walk and carry your backpack at the same time." I tell Hispanic parents, "Allow your children to do as many tasks as possible. Each task helps to birth a new **memory** cell each day."

CHAPTER 8
Food for Thought: The Brain and Food

In addition, a large and compelling body of research suggests that nutrition plays a major role in cognition, memory, moods, and behavior. Nutritional status is strongly correlated with a host of family and environmental variable, including socioeconomic status- likely to affect neurocognitive development.

— Eric Jensen

In my **parent engagement** training, it was important to explain to parents the need to pay attention to toxic materials and foods, both of which are critical factors to **brain** performance and their child's success.

I shared recently with a group of mothers how I walked into the cafeteria to see what they were serving for breakfast. It was Cocoa Puffs! What could the cafeteria manager be thinking? Chocolate and sugar, first thing in the morning for our kids' **brain**s? Chocolate and sugar do not relate to what I know about learning and the **brain**. The information about chocolate, like other toxic foods, is information we need to share with parents.

If parents are not cooking their own food, they will be serving fast foods with preservatives. Those preservatives affect children in different ways, from emotional fits to anger and moodiness. Many parents have no knowledge about how food affects their children's behaviors. The parents have told me that the kids just go wild and crazy at home. Frustrated and not knowing what else to do, they place their children in their rooms.

The kids are wild and crazy because the parents have not planned their day through by considering questions such as, "What did I give them to eat today? Did they have Cocoa Puffs or Fruit Loops in the morning? Was it sugar all day long? Did they drink chocolate or strawberry milk, Coke or Kool-Aid?" The food problem is not just diet deficiency, but also chemical preservative, carbohydrate, and sugar overload.

This is not to say that some of these things are not necessary, e.g., carbohydrates, in a good diet. However, the key is controlling excessive use of the things that can have negative impacts. For example, students' **brains** need some glucose to keep working, but the trick is to keep it at reasonable levels.

PRESERVATIVES

Preservatives are everywhere. Research indicates that environmental issues and preservatives affect our **brains**. Researchers have found that preservatives, such as salt (sodium) and sugar—found in foods such as chips and sweet drinks—are not healthy for brain development. It does not give the **brain** correct glucose for optimal school functioning.

I hear constantly from our Hispanic parents, many of whom have moved from island countries or from Central or South America, that they see a dramatic change in their children's behavior after they move to the United States. The families generally come from locations where they eat only natural foods. I suggest that their behavior change could be the effects of the foods they eat in the United States, most of which contain many preservatives. Sugary cereals and drinks, and chicken nuggets, have enormous amounts of preservatives for taste that affect children's nervous systems. It is said that if there were no sugar or salt in the foods, it would taste like cardboard.

Candy affects children's **brain**s dramatically. The dendrites connect in the **brain**, the candy or salt gets in the gap, or the synapse. Thinking slows. The **brain** connections, especially for **memory**, do not work. My children had to learn how to stop and wean themselves away from candy because I would not allow any of it in my classroom.

SKIM MILK

In one inner city school district, the mommies told me they were feeding their babies and toddlers skim milk because "I don't want them to be fat." It was important to listen and explain to them that cells of the **brain** and the cells of the nerves cannot grow without the natural fat of whole milk, and if a parent is decreasing the amount of natural fat, they are taking away the **brain**'s ability to develop and continue its growth process.

CAFFEINE

Caffeine is a strong brain stimulant, considered safe for most adults in small quality quantities, but caffeine is found in many of the foods and drinks that teens consumed daily. Too much caffeine causes insomnia, anxiety and nausea.

— David Sousa

During training, I help the parents see the correlation between caffeinated coffee drinks, tea, and sodas, and their children's behavior. Do not give soda to children because it contains a lot of sugar, which is detrimental to children's growing nervous systems. "But what about diet soda?" parents ask me.

Diet soda is toxic for children of all ages. The research demonstrates that children in middle school, drinking more than six to 10 diet sodas a day, turned the chemistry of their **brain**, over a determined time, into a chemical close to what we know as turpentine.

Some teens can also develop allergies to aspartame, the artificial sugar found in many diet sodas, and other food additives. This is what parents should know about artificial sugar. It causes:

- Hyperactivity
- Difficulty concentrating
- Headaches
- Inhibits physical growth

These are classic learning problems or issues that I have had to struggle with in the classroom. Parents struggle with these same problems and issues at home. Connections between artificial sugar and learning have to be taught to our Hispanic parents because the more foods containing preservatives that they give a child — such as giving them a chocolate mocha late in the day (which contains caffeine), the more liable they are to become hyperactive.

Section III
Parent Training

CHAPTER 9
Boots on the Ground:
Brain-Based Training in Action

Just like a city, the brain's overall operation emerges from the networked interaction of its innumerable parts....And so it is with the brain's operation: It doesn't happen in one spot, Just as in a city, no neighborhood of the brain operates in isolation. In brains and in cities, everything emerges from the interaction between residents, at all scales, locally and distantly.

— David Eagleman

It is my experience that school districts often find it difficult to know where to begin to engage parent stakeholders. In order to discover whether **brain-based** training can improve engagement between Hispanic parents and their ELL elementary-age children, I conducted a series of surveys to develop the pilot training and coaching program.

I recommend that administrators and coordinators take time to plan each step and, most significantly, know their parents from within the community.

A NEW PARENT PARADIGM

The **model** design was planned to build experiential learning around authentic intentional engagement by getting parents to participate in hands-on activities. The goal was to provide intentional, purposeful, and **engaged** educational experiences for Hispanic parents to enrich their role in the lives of their ELL elementary-aged children in the home, at school, and within the school community.

For the pilot program, **parent engagement** meant learning about **brain** functions and strategies to enhance those functions for parents of ELLs. The training program was intended to connect and bridge learning strategies from school to home in sustainable ways.

Based on 24 years of training sessions, evaluations, and my research study, my program design addresses the real needs and barriers experienced by today's parents with children in American public schools. They include:

1. How can I talk to my child's teacher more effectively?
2. How can I understand the directions on the homework?
3. How can I help my child to listen and follow directions more closely?

What resulted was a new paradigm of parent needs:

1. What is my purpose as a parent in my child's learning?
2. How will it meet the social responsibility of my child — especially with technology — in the future?
3. How do my emotions impact my purpose, and how do they impact my parent role and my family?

4. How does my learning as a parent create a cognitive impact on my children?

A PILOT WITH A PURPOSE: PARENT SUCCESS

By offering this uniquely designed pilot program, we had the direct experience of observing, analyzing, and video recording the thoughts, feelings, learning, perceptions, insights, and beliefs of 40 Hispanic parents as they completed the **brain-based** training program.

The pilot program took place in a south Texas border town. Researched and implemented in five urban school districts across the United States, the program **model** had not been implemented in border areas prior to the pilot program. My intent was to capture participant perceptions about the structured parent-training program to determine whether the strategies were useful and applicable to specific needs and growth when working with their children at home.

To launch the study, meeting with key administrators was essential. The purpose was to build a coalition of social capital with stakeholders within the schools and among the administration, and generate school community support for the program, in order to create a sustainable **model** and lay the groundwork for the parent training.

I know from leadership experiences that it is advantageous to establish positive dialogue with anyone invested in the success of students.

To ensure the pilot's success, all thinking and learning styles needed consideration to meet the needs of the Hispanic parents participating in the training.

Therefore, structures in the form of a **choreography** were set in place with purposeful tasks and timelines, specific to the desired goals, needs, and barriers of the parents in order to achieve successful outcomes.

BUILDING SOCIAL CAPITAL THROUGH AUTHENTICITY

Establishing authenticity ("a sense of self within self") was a priority. Did you know the word *authenticity* shares the same root word as *author*? This insight resonates with me as an author. It means that I bring my authentic self and my authentic experiences to these pages in order to share my ideas and give you a tried-and-true starting place to replicate and create your own authentic programs.

Building social capital with authenticity was critical to the first phase of the process. I held the stakeholder/parent meetings prior to designing and implementing the **brain-based** training program to help me learn, feel, and engage purposefully and comfortably with the stakeholders in a more natural and authentic way.

In order to communicate my passion for the training program to the parents during social capital building, at the initial meeting I shared the story of how my mother gave me a green tin frog when I became an entrepreneur and told me, "Jumping forward was the most important thing to know in life," because, biologically, frogs cannot jump backward. I held my tin frog as I welcomed the stakeholders to the team that only jumps forward!

My **Boots on the Ground** approach meant planning, scheduling, organizing, and defining the goals of the **brain-based** training program. To facilitate future replication of the pilot program meant looking at the total picture, which included all the planned details and dates sequenced logistically and aligned creatively.

CREATING A PATHWAY FOR THE BOOTS

To use of the Program Training Evaluation (PTE) analysis in the **Boots on the Ground** phase, the following procedures and steps required planning:

1. Arrange with administration for a parent orientation for two schools and invite parents to attend through marketing flyers and e-mails.
2. Gather and recruit the parent participants during the orientation.
3. Explain the **brain-based** training program to interested parents and inform them of what the training entails, answer questions, and obtain participation consent.
4. Secure translator services for training sessions.
5. Build social capital with the school district's parent coordinator through meetings and emails.
6. Arrange for training location and the use of technology, including video and audio equipment, and inform parents of dates, times, and locations of training. Personal phone calls to each participant are critical.
7. Arrange for childcare at training locations and ensure transportation and refreshments for parent participants.
8. Hold training sessions and follow-up sessions.
9. Conduct post-training interviews with participants to see what strategies were effective with their children.
10. Share results and conclusions with school administrators and stakeholders.

While recruiting the parent participants, it was crucial to ensure that their interest for engagement was coming from the heart and not for material gain or recognition. It was also essential to ensure that the same standards applied to the district stakeholders. Therefore, everyone involved had the opportunity to take the same survey, thus providing equal voice for all stakeholders.

ACCESSIBLE NETWORKS

In May 2015, a two-hour orientation for Hispanic parents of ELLs was held at the two selected schools and included questions, video sharing, and light refreshments. Out of 80 parents who attended, 66 attendees signed up and expressed an interest in participating in the training.

From the 66 parents who signed up, 40 Hispanic mothers were ultimately selected to be participants and attend the four-day, **brain-based** training, the follow up coaching session, and the final celebration with certificates. Final participation was based on the need for equal numbers from each school, having children in pre-K through Grade 4, participant availability for a five-day commitment, and subject to the principal's approval.

All participants were parents of ELL children enrolled in two of the poorest and lowest performing elementary schools in the district. All participants were mothers who had at least a middle school or high school education obtained in the United States or in Mexico, Honduras, or Guatemala.

SETTING THE TABLE

Food services and community resources were included so that all the physiological needs of the parents were met. It also ensured that they were able to engage fully in the training. Training for both schools was from 8:45 a.m. to 12:45 p.m. in a large, district-owned facility that was air-conditioned.

Mornings began with a breakfast beginning at 8:15 a.m., and lunch was provided at 12:45 p.m. Childcare for approximately 65 children of the parent participants was also provided.

We provided the meals for the parents and their children, and the school district provided childcare. The school district also provided eight parent liaisons and audio/technological equipment services.

Members of my training team included three facilitators and one technology specialist.

BEST PRACTICES

During the training, participants sat at round tables in groups of five to promote greater interaction and engagement. Each day, participants sat at different tables to create new parent teams and allow them to begin building their own community liaisons.

Rearranging the seating each day facilitated maximum exposure to other participants and encouraged discussion among the groups.

The **brain-based** training implemented through demonstration and **model**ing of intentional **scaffold**ing, **mediated** thinking, and learning processes and activities, facilitated parent learning. The **model**ing of strategies using all parts of the **brain** when working with children encouraged parents to share the thoughts, beliefs, ideas, and attitudes they experienced during the training.

A SENSE OF PURPPOSE

We had deep and passionate feelings about the goals, self-efficacy, hope, progressive engagement, and purposefulness toward the **brain-based** training program. Expressing those feelings helped the parents orient themselves, encourage each other, and build collaboration and cooperation.

Purposefulness is not just being, and not just doing. Specifically, it is how one acts and how one relates to the world. The underlying essential question of the study was whether the training would cultivate purpose and meaning enough to effect positive change in how Hispanic parents **engaged** with their children.

> *Purpose is the reason for which something is done or created or for which something exists. Purpose goes beyond serving others and indicates the search for a sense of community and the opportunity for self-expression and personal development.*
>
> — Aaron Hurst

It was our hope that themes, patterns, and insights into new and profound information about the **brain**, thinking, and learning strategies would help the Hispanic parents grow and establish more profound and meaningful relationships with their children, their children's teachers, and as a community of stakeholders.

CHAPTER 10
Parent Training

After all, despite some genetic pre-specification, nature's approach to growing a brain relies on receiving a vast set of experiences, such as social interaction, conversation, play exposure to the world, and the rest of the landscape of normal human affairs. The strategy of interaction, conversation, play, exposure to the world, and the rest of the landscape. The strategy of interaction with the world allows the colossal machinery of the brain to take shape from a relatively small set of instructions.

— David Eagleman

A real estate agent will tell you that real estate is all about location, location, location. Working with parents is all about training, training, training, and then more training. Throughout my years of experience serving school districts, I have discovered that parent thinking and learning is at the heart of any parent initiative. Without training in thinking and learning, however, there is no foundation for understanding, no dialogue, no trust in the short term, and certainly no long-term engagement.

Prior to my study, there were few to no **brain-based** training programs for Hispanic parents except for my own newly designed **model**. I wanted to prepare parents from lower socio-economic levels to apply thinking and learning skills and strategies at home to facilitate better thinking and learning processes in their children.

To my knowledge, there has not been a research study correlating the data between **parent engagement** and improved academic outcomes. Surely, I would want to be the one researcher to take that on.

English language learners continue to lag behind other student populations in academic achievement. It does not matter whether the community is largely Hispanic. Whatever language is being spoken, all parents need to learn that the first step to communicating with their children is consistency in logic and **scaffold**ing ideas rather than emotional response. This is an axiom that parents need to know for sure.

The **parent engagement** program for my study explored critical barriers and issues that normally prevented parents of ELLs from engaging fully in their children's education. What was also revealed, however, were three new 21st-century barriers: emotional investment of purpose, social capital building between schools, and cognitive impact.

COMMUNITY AND SCHOOL SETTING

The city in which the training took place was the second fastest-growing suburban center in the United States at that time. Located on the banks of the Rio Grande River, it was home to more than 250,000 residents. The district comprised more than 20 elementary schools that serviced more than 14,000 children.

From my viewpoint, the community and school district I selected for the study was representative of many of the Hispanic **communities** in this country, specifically given its geographical proximity to Mexico.

On a second level of selection refinement, I chose two of the elementary schools within the district to recruit parents of ELLs for **brain-based** training. I chose these schools based on the following criteria:

1. Willingness on the part of the school administrators to support the study.
2. Interest on the part of the parents of ELLs in kindergarten through Grade 4.
3. Parents' expectations of their role as it relates to their children's academic success.

The parent-training program included four days of hands-on training and three follow-up coaching sessions using meaningful, intentional **brain-based** concepts through **mediate** learning strategies expressed in a highly choreographed set of activities, videos, and discussion.

To keep the parents and the program on track, I needed a consistent level of precision scheduling and coordination, or what I like to call *choreography*.

The word **choreography** translates from two Greek words meaning, "to write the dance." I believe this captures exactly the approach needed to orchestrate a training session. It is a dance.

The impact of the training on **parent engagement** was evident in their changing roles as stakeholders in the **communities** and as willing thinking and learning coaches for their children. Results of this study indicated that parents found new purpose to build better relationships and increase engagement with their children and with the school through learned strategies.

I designed a training program that ran for four consecutive days in order to immerse parents in the new thinking and learning process, knowing that most parents in this community were able to make a four-day commitment to the study. After years of experience, I learned that four days was just enough to keep them learning and **engaged**. In addition, parents were required to attend a fifth day session within two months following the training to provide feedback, share what they learned, how they used it, and how their children grew from it.

For all parents, time of day was an important factor. From my years of experience, I knew that anywhere from four to five hours, complete with food and breaks, was the most optimal length of time to sustain intensity and interest.

Among our team members, Tuesday through Friday were the best days hold trainings. A designated person or coach within the district or within my team would call, email, and/or text all of the parents for reminders on Monday.

That way, we could ensure that everyone who signed up would show up on Tuesday morning. Knowing how many people were going to attend also gave us an accurate count to provide daycare in order to keep the participants totally focused.

An ideal maximum size for this kind of training is 75 participants. However, for this research project, I selected 40 committed research participants (20 parents from each of the two schools). I knew it was important to the research to have parents whom I knew would be fully committed. I also employed three trainers to assist so that the trainer-to-participant ratio was 1:10. This ratio was adequate for providing the necessary support for the parents.

The daily training centered on major thematic **scaffolds** about the **brain**. Each section was conducted with activities, a reflection with questions, dialogue within the teams, and then short research mini-lectures to support the activities and dialogue.

Through games, technology, cooperative learning, teamwork, and multi-modal activities, the training introduced new ideas and engaging ways for the parents to work with their children.

Parent reactions captured on video, questionnaires, surveys, focus groups, and interviews helped me to identify several structures of their beliefs.

THEMES OF MEANING

The **brain-based** training aligned units or themes of significance and meaning, each **scaffold**ing or building on the previous step. Within the themes were specific concepts connected for maximum learning. Each theme involved activities conducted by facilitators who helped the participants connect their thinking to parts of the **brain** during and after each activity. The following themes were covered:

Theme 1: The purpose and role of the parent with their child as it related to **brain** growth (various stages of **brain** development: intellectual, social, and emotional growth).

Theme 2: The purpose and role of the parent with their child relating to thinking and learning (parents, families).

Theme 3: How strategies and critical thinking can create a purpose in building **memory** and comprehension in their ELL children (better coaches of thinking and learning and homework).

Theme 4: How strategies and critical thinking can build planning and organizational skills (cognitive input).

Theme 5: The need for **brain-based** strategies that help children to think and learn more efficiently and proficiently in order to improve academics and with help at home (cognitive input).

Theme 6: With the use of their new knowledge and skills, parents become more powerful in helping their children and the neighbor's children in homework (social capital-building or responsibility).

Theme 7: Parents become more confident interacting with their child's school (social responsibility).

Theme 8: Parents begin to build social capital through teamwork, shared experiences, and confidence (social responsibility).

CHAPTER 11
Parent Marketing 101:
How to Fill a Room

Guerilla marketing dictates that you comprehend every facet of marketing, then employ with excellence the marketing tactics that are necessary.

— Jay Conrad Levinson

Your market is....the people around you have unmet needs. Identifying those unmet needs is your main task as a marketer.

— William Bridges

One of the most important aspects of my **parent engagement** training is the marketing effort that supports it. That is an E for Effort, an E for the Enthusiasm you will need to power the marketing process, plus the Energy level you will need to sustain momentum over a period of weeks.

Remember, the participating parents will naturally give you back all the energy you put into your marketing. The group energy of the parents who are learning during the training session will recharge your batteries.

Do not count on anything being "viral" these days. There is too much noise out there on social media. Emails go unread and sometimes end up in spam folders without the knowledge of both you and the recipient.

If you leave a message with someone at a residence, it may not reach its intended recipient or it may be inaccurate in the conveyance. Remember the old "telephone" game, where a simple message is whispered to the next person in line? The message becomes distorted with each retelling, and by the time it reaches the last person in line, it's a completely different message. This is how misinformation can spread.

I prefer to have a *direct phone or in-person conversation* with my prospective parents for the training. I listen and take notes regarding any obstacles that might prevent attendance at the training. If there is a widespread pattern of the same obstacle among my parents, I can probably address it and make procedural and substantive changes to eliminate or minimize the obstacle before the training starts. At the end of the day, marketing is largely about listening to and understanding the needs of consumers who will use your goods and services.

MARKETING ROLES

Marketing for a parent training is both task-oriented and creative in nature. Coordinators of parent training will be wearing a multitude of hats:

- Project manager
- Email list manager (Excel)
- Social media specialist (Facebook)
- Volunteer manager

- Artist/designer
- Writer
- Parent liaison between the school and the community
- Telemarketer

Identify your strengths on that list above, but also identify the gaps in your skill set or daily bandwidth. Just because you can handle a task does not mean you should, given your overall role of program coordinator. Don't be afraid to delegate!

For example, can a parent coordinator handle any of those roles on your behalf? Or a school volunteer? They do not have to be local!

For my Texas training, I had my contracted out-of-state language translator making phone calls to every parent. This freed up my time and allowed me to keep other aspects of the program in focus.

Plan the work, and work the plan, as they say. Start with the training date and work backwards several months, using the concept of the marketing funnel.

THE MARKETING FUNNEL

It helps to understand that marketing works like the funnel you use in your kitchen, wide at the top and narrow at the bottom. You start with a large number of **potential participants**, who become a smaller number of **prospective participants**, and finally, an even smaller number of **actual participants**.

In Texas, we started with an email list of several 100 potential parents with children in pre-K to fourth grade, from two schools, at the beginning of summer.

Eighty potential parents participated in an orientation session, where I presented the parent training engagement basics, along with a co-facilitator, Dr. Rodriguez. We refined our number to 60 prospective parents at the next meeting.

Then we began our "marketing conversion" blitz to get to our final group of 40 actual participants. That is how the marketing funnel works, communicating value at each point in the process until every one in your final group shows up on Day One of the parent training.

Here are the ingredients in my marketing recipe:

- Strong principals (who used All Call outbound messaging to communicate with prospective parents)
- Strong parent liaisons (who made phone calls)
- Emails
- Flyers and brochures
- Text, Dojo, and Remind technology capability
- A cell phone number list for calls and reminder texts
- Phone calls to every parent who expressed interest
- House visits with examples of course materials, such as the colorful backpacks we distributed to parents who participated
- Reminder phone calls to every parent, the day prior to the training

To this list, you can now add electronic invitations (E-invites) from providers such as Evite.com and Evensi.com, and Facebook, which allows you to create a unique Facebook page for each event. Here is an example of an Evite:

LOCATION AND LOGISTICS

I held my parent training at a civic center ballroom, large enough to accommodate our parents comfortably, as well as provide a separate room for their children.

I addressed all the transportation obstacles that might hinder participation. The civic center was in a central downtown location. We also provided bus transportation for parents and children at their respective schools, with morning pick-up and afternoon drop-off, all four days.

I hired eight teachers to head up the childcare, thus eliminating another parent worry. This is yet another reason to confirm your headcount for parent training, so you have the correct number of parents and children, and you provide sufficient transportation, meals and childcare.

FIVE FACEBOOK TIPS

1. Each Facebook post should have an engaging photograph or image accompanying it. A fun video is even better.
2. Keep your Facebook post content under 20 words. Facebook claims that maximum reader engagement happens at 40 characters (about seven words), and declines the longer your post reads.

3. Provide a hyperlink to the invitation landing page.
4. Make sure the "Share" feature is enabled.
5. Create a Facebook Event Page, if that will help.

MARKETING COMMUNICATION

When issuing an invitation to prospective participants, follow the who, what, when, where, why and how **Principle**:

- **Who:** What **communities** are you going to invite?
- **What:** What information are you going to engagement them in?
- **When:** Provide the day, date and time of the event.
- **Where:** Provide the location of the event, which should be near a bus line. Be sure to include clear directions and parking information.
- **Why:** State the intention of the event with just enough information to pique interest and convince them of the value of the event.
- **How:** Explain how the program will benefit their children's learning.

Make sure communications to parents are clear, concise, and compelling.

Short, simple, and direct sentences are preferable. Long sentences with clauses and excessive formality inhibit comprehension by the reader. Make each sentence conversational, like you are actually speaking to each parent in a relaxed setting with no interruptions!

It is permissible to use one-sentence paragraphs because the white space around it will emphasize a key point. If possible, avoid using ALL CAPS and excessive exclamation points. Parents want to be talked to, not yelled at.

Test the email subject line with your parent coordinators, or an actual prospective parent, to see if it is something they would respond to in the flood of incoming emails.

Congratulations! You can add Event Marketing to your skill set!

CHAPTER 12
Designing Welcoming Environments

...the entire sensory environment is packaging for any specific issue or content with which we are faced...context is meaningful and affects us whether or not we are consciously aware of the consequences.

— Caine & Caine

Participation is a two-way boulevard. We ask for parent participation, and when it does not occur or occur to the levels we expect, we wonder why it happened. A better way to look at this issue is from the provider point of view. It may have nothing to do with your parents.

"If you build it, they will come," is the oft-quoted line from the 1989 movie, *Field of Dreams*. It is a false premise. The parents may come to our "field of **parent engagement** training" begrudgingly if forced, or they may not come at all.

First of all, schools are welcoming environments because they provide a service of teaching and learning for your children. That is your foundation.

Second, I have seen devoted teachers do nothing but give their time and energy to helping your children in these schools. The environment is already there in terms of teachers of the students.

The parents are hesitant to become **engaged** because they do not know what it is they are becoming **engaged** in. They may not have the English language in order for them to understand and comprehend. They may not understand how warming and welcoming a training session will be.

All those doubts and questions will be part of the development of your program, including the marketing of the program, which goes back to our Boots on the Ground concept. Here is how I designed outreach for one parent training program in a major city in the center of the country that happened, at that time, to be the fifth largest school district in the country.

First, the teachers held a meeting to determine the messaging they needed to get the parents to come to the training. Because there was no social media at the time, we determined that house-to-house calls would need to be made. We would not let the teachers go out into the neighborhoods individually. Instead, they went out in teams of three, and they went to every school and sat with the parents, showing them the backpack of materials they were going to receive if they participated.

The teachers left flyers containing all the pertinent information about the program and told the parents they would be calling them later as a follow-up. If the parent needed a ride to attend, we told them we had somebody who would pick them up. It was like a get-out-the-vote effort, giving voters rides to the polls.

Each year our training was held in a different location, and we had buses to pick up parents and their children at school sites. If parents were coming to the training from one of the three school sites, there was a bus there to pick them up in the morning.

If they could not get there, we made calls to people who could give these parents a ride to the training. These are the mission-critical strategies of going out into your community in a grassroots fashion and removing the transportation obstacle. The parents appreciate that gesture.

In addition, we provided meals and childcare. If you can feed them and take care of their children, the parents can concentrate on the **brain-based** themes.

As I mentioned earlier, you need to know your nexus. This is why we like to train parents with children in pre-K, kindergarten, and grades one and two. More than likely, those parents are also going to have other children in higher grades or children who are much younger.

Let me say something about gender. In my experience with heavily Hispanic districts, most everything is geared toward the mother. In this culture, the fathers most likely work. Moms do not generally work outside of the home, and they can participate during the day if you provide childcare.

Know your nexus. Survey your parents and listen to what they tell you formally and informally. Observe them in both the orientation sessions and in the actual training.

Are they interested? Are they asking questions? Are they having fun while they learn? These are the keys to engagement.

Do not just build the perfect program and expect 100% parent participation. Build a solid program using guidance from this book and guidance from your school leadership. Then modify it from the feedback you receive from the parents. They will tell you what they are thinking. Let the parents help you build that *Field of Dreams* that naturally attracts the next wave of participation.

CHAPTER 13
Engagement Strategies

People usually consider walking on water or in thin air a miracle. I think the real miracle is to walk on earth. Every day we are engaged in a miracle which we don't even recognize: a blue sky, white clouds, green leaves, the curious eyes of a child—our own two eyes.

— Thich Nhat Hanh

Speaking of miracles ...

Bringing together 40 participants for four days of training means the participants all need to be on the same page. Even if they live in the same community or are parents of children at the same school, you cannot assume they know each other or know each other well, especially because their children are in grades pre-K through four.

I cannot overstate the importance of engagement strategies for a parent-training program like this. We made sure to choreograph our **parent engagement** down to each minute of the day.

ICEBREAKERS

Each day began with a 20-minute icebreaker. In addition to helping participants get to know each other, these icebreakers had another purpose. They helped the parents disengage from the world outside and focus on the day ahead.

One example of an effective icebreaker is to form a Circle of Knowledge (COK). Each participant talks to their partner or the person next to them, sharing information and communicating things they like.

A variation of the COK icebreaker is to communicate a message about the **brain**. Using string, we connected everyone's hands in the circle with string and demonstrated to them the way that neurons and dendrites connect.

With two trainers in the room, one trainer can lead the icebreaker from the front, and the other trainer can serve as the assistant and roam the room.

Sometimes I would lead the icebreaker to **model** and give my own personal message to the parents.

VIDEOS AND JOURNAL ENTRIES

Handpicked videos, presented at the conclusion of each section, created and developed discussion points for parents to ponder and reflect on.

To accompany the first video, *The Watchful Guardians of Apricot Lane Farms*, parents received a highly creative magnet as a symbol of partnership in the family.

For the second video, *A Pig Named Emma, 13 Piglets and 1 Big Miracle*, parents received a tile plaque symbolizing their role as steadfast caretakers with a sense of purpose.

Finally, to illustrate the role of special relationships and partnerships within a family, parents received a hand-crocheted rooster in a box with a ribbon signifying parental love and nurturing, and the building of safety, security, and relationship with their children. A journal writing assignment followed the video screenings:

Day One Assignment
1. What is process?
2. How does the **brain** process information?

Day Two Assignment
1. What is a barrier?
2. What is security?
3. Why is technology a barrier to engaging with children?

Day Three Assignment
1. What is strategy?
2. Why do strategies help our children think better?

Day Four Assignment
1. As a parent, how can I be better **engaged**?
2. After each activity, mini-lecture, and video, participants were encouraged to share their thoughts together as a team.
3. What did they like?
4. What was meaningful?
5. What did they think?

All facilitators listened, and as the tech specialist wrote out the thoughts on the screen, everyone could see the teams and their meaning and purpose coming together.

Choreography is a bit like egg salad.

— Susan F. Tierno

DR. SUE'S EGG SALAD RECIPE

This healthy egg salad is such an easy lunch recipe for kids who just read *Because of Winn Dixie*. This example of American cuisine feeds 16 hungry second graders.

Ingredients

- 20 hardboiled eggs, chopped into small pieces
- 3/4 cup celery, diced (about 3-4 medium stalks)
- 1/4 cup red onion, grated (like cheese)
- 5 medium dill pickles, finely diced (Kids love pickles!)
- 2 giant squeezes of regular yellow mustard
- 4 shakes of paprika
- 4 shakes of ground pepper
- 3 shakes of sea salt, to taste (I always explain why Kosher salt is best for them)

Instructions

1. Boil the eggs. Carefully drain the water and run the eggs under cool water before peeling. I let them sit in the refrigerator overnight for easiest peeling.
2. Chop eggs, celery, onion and pickle as noted and place everything in a bowl.
3. Add in mustard, paprika, pepper. Mix with a big wooden spoon until combined. Taste and season with salt as desired.
4. Spread on fresh bread. Put on paper plate. Serve with a big handful of potato chips. Watch movie, *Because of Winn Dixie,* and ENJOY!

CHAPTER 14
Choreography

Many of today's motion pictures are made on a 21-day shooting schedule. The reason for this involves the budget for the film and the limited availability of the acting talent. Given the compressed timeline, the movie producers must assemble all the elements (including the director, actors, camera crew, set builders, makeup and wardrobe personnel, and the caterer) in one central location. Every hour of every day is scripted just like the movie. It is intentional and disciplined. There is no room for error.

To keep my parent training sessions on schedule, I applied a **"Choreography** of Activities" document, which I share with you on the following pages. If you look closely, you will see that each day is segmented into 30-minute blocks, and with my trainers, I had those 30-minute blocks divided up even more precisely. Each day had its own detailed **choreography** coordinating these elements:

1. Time
2. Goals

3. Objectives
4. Facilitators
5. Materials

Note that each 30-minute block is marked by an Activity Code that tracks the type of activities that will allow for different types of learning:

- **Active Learning**: Learning by doing
- **Emotional Learning:** Videos and reflections
- **Engagement:** Caring and being cared about
- **Thinking Engagement:** Dialoguing about and engaging the participants in an idea, a focus, a dialogue or an insight or belief.

Activity Codes

TAC = Tactile

T = Technology

L = Listen-Lecture

K = Kinesthetic

A/V = Auditory-Visual

TnT = Turn n' Talk

W = Writing

EC = Emotional Connection

GW = Group or Team work on/or with manipulatives

Time	Day 1	Day 2	Day 3	Day 4
8:15-8:40	Sign In and Breakfast	Sign In and Breakfast	Sign In and Breakfast	Sign In and Breakfast
8:40-9:00	Opening ICEBREAKER	Opening ICEBREAKER	Opening ICEBREAKER	Opening ICEBREAKER
9:00-9:30	Opener Make-a-Plan (MAP) The what and why of steps Make-A-List (MAL) of all items in Thinkparents are powerful-PAC™ *TAC, K, W*	Opener Apple Activity Tools for Parents T-Chart *TAC, K*	Opener Are We There Yet? Map Activity *K, TnT, GW*	Opener eBook Reading e-Connecting to Literacy *T, A/V*
9:30-10:00	**Kahoot-It** An online quiz on parents' perspective on the role of parenting and setting the purpose of the parent seminar *T, A/V*	**Parent Roles** Revisit Key Questions: • What was school like for me? • What do I want school to be like for my children? • As a parent, what role do I want to play in my children's school environment and learning process? *EC (VIDEO TEAMS)*	**Different Ways of Connecting** The four categories of the (MBTI) study will be discussed and connected with the brain's different KEY styles of sorting, resorting and prioritizing Why is sorting, resorting and prioritizing important to our children and thinking? *Play Game; TAC, GW*	**Think-Coaching for Home Practice!** Revisit different strategies used throughout the program MAP MAL Word strategies with pads and list of words Dictionary.com *T, W* ROLL the dice story cubes Bridging Cards™ *TAC, TnT* *TEXT a sentence*
10:00-10:10	**MINI-BRAIN BREAK**	**MINI-BRAIN BREAK**	**MINI-BRAIN BREAK**	**MINI-BRAIN BREAK**
10:10-10:30	**Meet the Brain** Different parts of the brain and their functions, and the role of	**Brain Connection & Patterns** Parents will connect the parts of the brain and	**Dendrites** Video: "The Alzheimer's Brain" The role of brain	**Think ABOUT IT!** Introduce the scaffolded 6 steps to building a project

	cognitive function and dysfunction Left-Right frontal and back of brain How to use each part GAME OF NADA "input-elaboration-output" *L, TnT*	their functions using a 3-D model of the brain GAME: Tables with brain parts will get up and go find the other brain parts to make a whole brain *TAC, K*	development vis-à-vis critical, creative, and emotional thinking How can you help your child as a parent? *TnT, TEXT a message*	Using it all from Right Brain to Left Brain frames to decision making with *Let's ThinkWrite*™ *TAC, K, A/V*
10:30-11:00	**ACTIVITIES** *Make-a-Brain hat/puzzle* *Play game* *K*	**ACTIVITIES** *Brain puzzle* *Tripods & brain information* *TAC, GW*	**ACTIVITIES** *Make a bridge with popsicle sticks* *Text-Your-Thinking as it Happens* *TAC, K*	**ACTIVITIES** *Let's Apply It Strategies from Above* *TAC, K, A/V*
11:00-11:30	**Brain Connection** Explore the role of dendrites in brain function and its implications with children's responses to the environment "Radio Brain" *AV, TnT*	**Preparing the Brain for School** Parents become experts of the different stages of brain development *GW, TnT*	**Be a Parent Coach** *4 Parts of Powerful Parenting* • Provide basic needs • Provide safety & security • Provide love • Be a Process Coach and a Strategy Coach What is Thinking? *TnT*	**Then What?** *Input-Elaboration-Output* Elaborate on the steps in the Let's ThinkWrite™ Project-Based Learning *TAC, K*
11:30-11:45	**ACTIVITIES** *Dendrites Spider Web* *Dendrites Cut-Out* *K, TAC*	**ACTIVITIES** *Make-A-Menu* *TAC, K, W, GW*	**ACTIVITIES** *Mind Mapping and Making Decisions Using Theme Cards* *TAC, A/V*	**ACTIVITIES** *Team PBL Project on the theme of "Dinosaurs"* *GW*
11:45-12:00	Video: "The Guardians" Journal Writing	Video: "Emma" Journal Writing	Video: "The Pig & the Rooster: An Unlikely	Video: "ThinkParents ARE POWERFUL

		"What is *process*?" "How does the brain process information?"	"What is **barrier**?" "What is security?" "Why is technology a barrier to engaging children?"	*Relationship*" Journal Writing "What is *strategy*?" Why do strategies help your children think better?"	*2015"* Journal Writing MindMeister "How can you be better engaged as a parent?"
		W	W	W	W
12:00-12:30		**FOCUS GROUP**	**FOCUS GROUP**	**FOCUS GROUP**	**FOCUS GROUP**
12:30		**Lunch**	**Lunch**	**Lunch**	**Lunch**

CHAPTER 15
A Fresh Approach:
Structured Mediated Learning

My method involves not just making you know something in a passive way, but how to produce it, how to create it. I am not just passing to you information, but passing to you all that you need to know in order to be able to learn by yourself.

— Dr. Reuven Feuerstein

One of the pillars supporting **brain-based** learning as a training approach is the concept and application of Structured **Mediated** Learning (SML) or **Mediated** Learning Experience (MLE). **Mediated** learning experience is the intentional processing of procedures, information, and the output of thinking that must be processed in order to function in the world. Mediation stresses the communal understanding of knowledge, collaborative sharing of experience, and the sorting or categorizing of ideas. The mediator helps the learner frame, filter, and schedule stimuli, and ultimately influences the potential ways that transfer of knowledge occurs in the student's thinking.

SAME CULTURE, DIFFERENT LEARNING APTITUDES

Dr. Reuven Feuerstein developed the theory of **Mediated** Learning in the 1950s as a way to explain how individuals learn differently. It began with a cultural observation. Feuerstein noticed that adults emigrating to Israel's highly technologically-driven society from different cultures demonstrated varying levels of learning when adapting to their new home. Some variations were explained by the original culture of the immigrants. What Feuerstein found more fascinating was the difference in learning aptitude for individuals from the same culture. What accounted for this difference?

The underachievers had not learned to learn. If someone cannot adapt to a more complex, new way of living, it is not a sign of that individual's lack of intelligence, but a **modification** that requires the use of cognitive tools. I find a similarity in our own country, where we assimilate many newcomers and expect them to have brought with them the learning processes needed to navigate our educational system as parents and as students.

Feuerstein built and replicated an entire body of research. Hundreds of papers have examined **Mediated** Learning's relationship with cognitive science and neuroscience. Moving beyond theory and practice at an individual level, the **Mediated** Learning field now looks at the **systems** we can design to allow individuals to be more adaptable in new cultural environments. To this end, I fully integrate the principles of **Mediated** Learning into my daily instruction and my **parent engagement** training and approach. It is woven into my **choreography** of activities and cadence of interaction with both students and parents.

MEDIATION CRITERIA

Mediated Learning is a portal to develop interactional skills, encourage autonomous learning, and metacognition (or "thinking about thinking"). Deployed to detect and assess a student's strengths and weaknesses, it offers strategies to remediate thinking dysfunction, and in some cases, unleash a student's potential.

Feuerstein identified 10 criteria essential to mediation:

1. Intentionality and Reciprocity
2. Meaning
3. Transcendence
4. Competence
5. Self-Regulation
6. Sharing
7. Individuation
8. Goal Planning
9. Challenge
10. Self-Change

There is only a small bit of elaboration in this chapter, but I would invite you to learn about these criteria in more depth in *Mediated Learning: In and Out of the Classroom* (Skylight, 1996).

Mediation is a flexible and open approach, with the opportunity to personalize the application **scaffold** and the key concepts.

How It Works

Mediated Learning involves the use of a **mediated** learning coach, who can be a parent, sibling, teacher, or other professional closely involved in the learner's life. The mediator is someone who transforms and organizes the various stimuli experienced in the environment to the learner.

MLE is often associated with *working memory* (how we hold **memory** in place and think in terms of next steps).

This is especially helpful for students who cannot hold one thought in their mind, let alone multiple thoughts, at one time.

Feuerstein identified three main areas where the mediating coach can influence a student:

1. Input
2. Process/Elaboration
3. Output

For example, an **input** strategy might involve the teacher saying to a student, "Look at the board or look at the book and tell me what it says," prompting a gathering of information (through the ears and eyes). This mentoring, or mediating, is meant to counter a student who rushes into a task, resulting in careless mistakes and delays.

An example of **elaboration** could be an elementary grade social studies class, where students are taught how to use the glossary, including where a glossary is located in a book, plus the concepts of ABC order, guide-words, and definitions.

The **output** phase is associated with a solution or product. An output example might be, "Take the words of the week and put them in ABC order."

A Powerful Approach

Mediated Learning is applicable to all age groups, so I can use it with both my parents and my students, as well as my friends outside the training! It is individualized to the learner, creating a custom process, which is immediately supportive in nature. No one is grouped in with the others and feeling lost. It is attuned to cognitive development, which implies personal growth. It even allows learners to go beyond the learning at hand and think about their thinking. It embraces new experiences and encourages integration into the learning process.

CHAPTER 16
Brain-Based Activities

You might think that who we are as adults is now fixed in place, immovable. But it's not: in adulthood our brains continue to change. Something that we shaped—and can hold that shape—is what we describe as plastic. And so it is with the brain, even in adulthood: experience changes it, and it retains the change.

— David Eagleman

At the core of the parent training, I designed a series of **brain-based**, supported training activities. The themes that emerged from the training activities and materials for parents came from the use of hands-on activities, a full technology presentation for visual impact, and more than 18 intentional and interactive activities that included games, dialogue, five videos, and structured team reflections.

In my experience, training parents is quite different from teaching children. My recipe for training parents covers three approaches:

1. **Brain-Based Learning**
2. **Mediated Learning, or How to be a Think-Coach**
3. **Social Emotional Learning**: How to talk so kids will think and think so kids will talk

All three approaches are featured in this book.

I always make sure that I choreograph for purpose, participation and interaction. For my team of trainers, it is an intentional, purposeful breakdown of physiological, intellectual, emotional, and chronological elements. All of this is planned before training begins.

Four facilitators led the activities described below and resulted in learned experiences for the parents.

Each activity is interconnected to one or more of the parts of the **brain** and builds comprehension.

As a trainer and choreographer, it is imperative for you to know the parts of the **brain**. As shown in the **brain** stage graphics in Chapter 4, I explain visually and verbally during all activities that the **brain** is massive in its complexity and capabilities. The **brain** deals with every part of what we do, from the time we are born through old age.

The remainder of this chapter is an extensive resource for **parent engagement** and includes 18 **activities** described at length. These activities are at the heart of the parent training I conducted and on which I based my research.

I think you will find these activities extremely valuable, and your parents will find them informative and enjoyable. They will also gain a lot of knowledge, skills, and understanding about how their children's **brain**'s work.

Activities are at the heart of learning.

Each one of the following activities was organized and used during the training. Every activity is simply described here and outlines how the **brain** works when the activity is in process. Reactions and input from parents is also described.

ACTIVITY 1: APPLE PEEL

ACTIVITY: Parents are asked to find out the best "tool" to peel an apple. Three people are asked to come up to the front. Three different tools are given. The purpose of the activity is to demonstrate the inferential thinking of giving their children the best tools to make a decision and connect their thinking well.

BRAIN ACTIVITY: This activity connects the prefrontal cortex to thinking, planning, problem solving, and the sensory (strip) cortex where current information is integrated into emotion and **memory**.

This **brain** activity and reaction is then connected to the motor (strip) cortex, which plays a critical role in initiating muscle action to arm and hand muscles required to use the tool to peel the apple. The muscle action is then connected to the amygdala, which has the ability to generate positive emotion with the perception and thought of the activity.

INSIGHTS: Parents noted, insightfully, that the activity was a way for them to understand that they need the right strategies for their learning in order to help their children learn. Comments included, "I learned that you can have some problem, and you may not have the right strategies, but you will always find something," and "About the apples, that gives us strategies [it taught us] to be prepared as moms so we can help our children … It was really helpful."

This comment in particular indicated that this parent participant recognized the need to know, understand, and apply strategies.

ACTIVITY 2: BRAIN HATS

ACTIVITY: In this activity, parents are asked to hold, touch, and feel a lifelike **brain** made of soft rubber. This includes examining the texture of the rubber **brain** and its different parts. The intention of this activity is for the participants to use their hands and eyes to help them become better informed about the parts of the **brain**.

BRAIN ACTIVITY: Engaging in such an activity helps to interconnect the occipital lobe, which processes visual information and relays the sensory information to the cortex. Touching the rubber **brain** allows participants to get a sense of what the **brain** form is like.

Parents are then given a **brain** hat that requires assembly before wearing. This exercise requires the connection of the occipital lobe and its use of spatial relationship to the prefrontal cortex that handles thinking and planning, organizing, and problem solving.

These three thinking skills are located in the prefrontal cortex and emphasized by the activity's facilitator as being critical to organizing all bits of information that enters a human's **brain**.

This activity helps demonstrate to parents how intentional and masterful they need to be in working with their children in thinking and planning, organization, and problem-solving skills.

In addition, the activity demonstrates that by using the sensory cortex or the tactile sensation of the hands while touching the parts of the rubber **brain**, the participants could begin to understand the organ called a **brain**. It demonstrates to them how their children take in information, think, and learn. As parents, they realize the sense of how powerful the **brain** is and how much it can accomplish in a short amount of time when given the right direction and connections.

INSIGHTS: Parents expressed overwhelming appreciation for this hands-on activity. Each wore their **brain** hat for at least an hour during the training and made comments such as, "I really learned how my child's **brain** works."

One parent noted that being more organized and understanding strategies or activities that emphasize this would help her be more patient with her children. All the facilitators observed that the parent participants were becoming knowledgeable quickly, making each activity more productive in learning the inferential message about the **brain**.

ACTIVITY 3: BRAIN PUZZLES

ACTIVITY: Parents are asked to cut, color, and mark parts of the **brain** (as shown in Chapter 6) to create puzzle pieces. They are then asked to assemble the pieces without seeing the whole **brain**. With the puzzle pieces scattered on tables throughout the room, participants interact in a kinesthetic activity that requires them to locate other individuals in the room who have the various puzzle parts of the **brain** they need.

Parents then form teams and put their **brain** puzzle together as a whole **brain**.

BRAIN ACTIVITY: This activity interconnects the occipital lobe, which processes visual information and its myriad characteristics. The occipital lobe is connected to the parietal lobe that not only synthesizes information, but also processes distance, size, shape, intensity and location.

INSIGHTS: Parents overwhelmingly favored the puzzle activities, as evidenced in their faces as they did the activities, **model**ed their hats, interacted to share what they liked the best, and commented.

One parent expressed positively, "I love these activities so much [not just because of the organization but], there are so many ways [that you have shown us] how to help our children that we were not aware of."

ACTIVITY 4: CIRCLE OF KNOWLEDGE

ACTIVITY: This activity is conducted to engage the group of participants during the follow-up coaching sessions. The purpose of this activity is to recall and organize factual information about the **brain**.

Parents are asked to form a large circle in order to face one another. Two rubber **brains** are distributed, one at either end of the circle. Each parent passes the **brain** and says one fact that they remember about the **brain**. Music is played as the rubber **brains** are passed around.

When the music stops, parents are asked to gather in teams of four and talk about their facts and ideas.

BRAIN ACTIVITY: This activity involves engaging various parts of the **brain**, such as the parietal lobe that synthesizes information as it relates to the body and its physical self.

Although synthesizing is relaying information, the frontal lobe is drawn into the activity by interconnecting the muscles that capture the rubber **brains** as they are passed, using both sides of the body.

This interconnection relays to the mid**brain**, or the area of the **brain** that transmits both auditory and visual information; the hind**brain** controls the body as the mid**brain** relays the information.

As the participants hear music, their **brains'** temporal lobe areas are **engaged**, which restructures **memory** and interprets music.

INSIGHTS: Many comments from the parents were insightful, but one particular comment captured how all of the parents collectively felt as they listened, moved, and actively shared in this activity. This comment in particular indicated that the participant recognized that she "was not informed about how all the things [the parts of] the **brain** can ... work."

ACTIVITY 5: CIRCLE OF KNOWLEDGE AND DENDRITE CONNECTIONS

ACTIVITY: Parents form a circle with their hands in the air. The hands held high around the circle are meant to simulate dendrites, or neurons, in the **brain**.

The purpose is to demonstrate visually and in a tactile and kinesthetic way what occurs literally as thinking is relayed, transferred, and interconnected to map **brain** activity.

It is meant to teach participants that each dendritic growth happens due to the process of connection in thinking steps. The more neurons fired off, the better the thinking occurs.

Colored yarn may be used to demonstrate how the dendrites reach out to various parts of the **brain**. As this is narrated, the yarn is connected to the hands held high in the air.

BRAIN ACTIVITY: This activity involves the occipital lobe that relays sensory information to the cortex and processes the visual information that is then interconnected to the prefrontal cortex to ensure thinking. The information then continues on to the hippocampus in the **brain** that collects the received visual and verbal information and turns it into **memory**.

INSIGHTS: Parent comments on this activity demonstrated emotion. They were overwhelmed that they could, in fact, learn from the process of such an interactive activity.

One participant noted, "I am surprised at the amount of information I have learned ... that means [that my child can learn] and store a lot of information."

ACTIVITY 6: MAKE-A-PLAN

ACTIVITY: The purpose of this activity is to demonstrate and ensure the parents learn that organization in the **brain** requires intentional thinking, not action or reaction.

The **brain** works more efficiently if organizational or procedural steps are taken. The intention is to engage the participants using a tactile strategy. This means that participants have to both visually and with their hands touch the parts of the **brain** that interconnect for more organized thinking.

Once this concept is learned, the three-word procedural steps of First, Next, and Last is taught to the participants. Each parent writes the three words in boxes.

To help emphasize the organizational process, all participants are given some direction words, such as cut, get, write, color, or do, that they sort and put into order under the categories of First, Next, and Last to create logical steps to complete a task.

These words are given in order to demonstrate the quick and efficient use of **memory** and its use in order to complete both directional tasks in the house and to complete a task such as homework. Once the steps are introduced and learned by the participants, this strategy is used thereafter for every task in the training.

BRAIN ACTIVITY: The strategy draws upon the use of the hippocampus, the part of the **brain** that receives information and works at turning short-term **memory** into long-term **memory**. This action is then relayed to the temporal lobe where the information is restructured for permanent **memory**.

INSIGHTS: The parents were excited as they learned this strategy and applied it. They understood clearly several impactful and efficient concepts. One parent noted, "The 3-step rules [First, Next, Last] are very creative and less harsh on our children to finish their tasks."

Another mother expressed the overall impact in a statement of gratitude: "I love how [the facilitator] has taken this much devotion in improving the encouragement of parents to help their children educate themselves. Her passion is so strong that it shows, and it can't help but touch us all. Every mother I see in trainings has changed from one day to the next."

The idea of talking to, yelling at, acting, and reacting to their children to get them to work on their homework was felt in a realization articulated by another participant, who commented, "I now understand that giving my kids many choices are not good. When doing homework I will make a plan—First, Next, Last."

ACTIVITY 7: BASEBALL GAME

ACTIVITY: The intention of this activity is reflection and sharing of ideas, but in a more sports-like activity. The object is for parents to find three people with whom to share ideas about the information they have just learned.

I want to create pattern repetition in a more kinesthetic way and to demonstrate how to create pattern repetition to build **memory**.

The parents each receive three colored cards that contain questions. They then move among four areas of the room marked like the bases on a ball field.

At each base, participants discuss with others the ideas and concepts that they have learned in the training that pertain to the question cards. They also record others' responses to the questions. A whistle blows to mark the end of the discussion at each base.

Once the final round, or home run, is completed, the participants discuss all three of the questions and responses. They then synthesize and share their summaries with the whole training group.

BRAIN ACTIVITY: Organization requires the use of the frontal lobe, which is located just above and within the wrinkles of the prefrontal cortex. This is generally termed the executive function center, which creates planning for the activity, and then, organizing and thinking about what to say during the activity.

INSIGHTS: It was very clear from parent comments that the interaction, sharing, and dialogue were helpful to them as learners.

Various comments included, "I liked the exercise about communicating with others," and "I learned to listen, organize, and interchange opinions." This activity demonstrated, and was recognized by the parents, that organization is a skill that can be learned and applied in creative ways.

ACTIVITY 8: MARBLES

ACTIVITY: The object of the game of marbles is to have parents work in teams and organize themselves to create rules and play some form of marbles. The **brain** has its own endurance for origination and innovation when it comes to activities. The intention of the game of marbles is to liken scattering marbles to the thoughts and events that occur throughout daily life. For parents, it is dealing with their young children. In other words, thoughts and events that are difficult to control, and result in chaos, often replace structure and order.

Parents discuss the rules and devise strategies to hit other marbles. In doing so, they consider and apply problem-solving, rule-making, and decision-making skills.

BRAIN ACTIVITY: These skills require the use of the interconnection of the **brain**'s frontal lobe (that uses opposite sides of the body and plans for the future) with the parietal lobe that processes distance, size, shape, intensity, and location. These parts of the **brain** are interconnected to the hind**brain** that controls the body and muscle function and coordination.

The purpose of the marbles game is to correlate, or interrelate, both multi-sensory objects with focused thinking. Focused thinking connects old ideas with new ideas and helps determine what errors to avoid. The movement of marbles in all directions is often times out of control, much like the **brain** under the stress of receiving too much information, which can overwhelm the processing ability.

The game of marbles literally connects the cognitive skills of the cerebellum, the spatial relation skills of the occipital lobe, and the processing of rules, or emotional **memory**. The **brain** is not designed to multitask, which is the reason for a clear set of rules for the game.

INSIGHTS: One insightful parent noted, "The marbles [showed us that] we cannot control everything at the same time." She added that she thought the game helped her realize she must control herself and then her kids by getting organized and setting rules.

Another mother expressed that she realistically saw herself, during her day's activity, acting the way the marbles moved. This demonstrated a profound level of learning and application to change for her.

Using the frontal lobe for goals and planning. I designed fun game-playing strategies to help them learn about motor skills and spatial relationships.

ACTIVITY 9: DRA. WRIGHT

ACTIVITY: The intention of this large circle activity is to build on the Circle of Knowledge and engage the participants in a funny story that involves directionality. While a facilitator reads a story and stops at each of the direction words, emphasizing which direction, the participants pass the rubber brain to each other and follow the directions in the Dra. Wright story.

BRAIN ACTIVITY: By following directions and paying attention to left/right directionality cues, the participants draw upon the temporal lobe intentionally (for short-term **memory**) and the occipital lobe and thalamus that quickly relays sensory information to the cortex for decision-making.

INSIGHTS: Parent comments were similar to those made about the Circle of Knowledge in that they did not realize the importance of listening and thinking simultaneously and intentionally. What they realized is that, oftentimes, upon hearing a direction, the **brain** processes the information in the opposite way.

Although this was humorous emotionally, once related to the real world, the parents realized the mistakes that could be made in this way with their children or their family.

ACTIVITY 10: JACKS

ACTIVITY: Parents form teams of two, three, or four with a bag of jacks and a rubber ball. They are asked to create their own rules based on Jacks rules they used as children. They apply the input-elaboration-output concept during the activity and conceptualized strategies to win while working on motor skills and spatial relationships. They discover how jacks fall on the ground in direction-close or clustered, far, and near patterns.

Parents are allowed to text their thoughts throughout the game, or they may document their ideas in a text dialogue.

One person from each team is designated to handle the texting and writing.

BRAIN ACTIVITY: Similar to marbles, the game of jacks required the use of both the frontal lobe for goals and planning execution once the ball is in the air, and the use of the occipital lobe for processing distance and location. Once relayed to transmitters in the hind**brain**, the muscle coordination with the thinking takes place.

INSIGHTS: Parents commented that they had not played the game in quite some time. This caused a great deal of chaos in terms of coordinating to throw the ball into the air and gathering a given number of jacks. Parents noted overall that the game required a great deal of thinking ahead, and they discussed how it related to their learning and their children's thinking and learning.

ACTIVITY 11: RADIO BRAIN

ACTIVITY: The purpose of this listening and speaking activity is to interpret and synthesize the meaning of a sound as it relates to the participants' children.

A two-minute audio of radio channels being changed in a car demonstrates that the on-and-off quality of what the **brain** captures and processes is very inconsistent. The two-minute audio causes participants to laugh, especially if one of the facilitators acts out a child who has a **brain** that could have been functioning like the audio recording.

BRAIN ACTIVITY: Using the emotion generated in the amygdala, the part of the **brain** that generates the emotion from perception and thought, participants use technology (mobile devices) to receive the audio recording of the radio to take home and play for their spouse.

INSIGHTS: Parents appeared particularly motivated to learn the phenomenon of the changes in their children's **brains**, which they expressed in various comments. "To me it was the radio that [demonstrated how] we sometimes [try to] do [too] many things during the day, and sometimes we don't realize what we are doing," one parent stated. Another participant pondered that statement and expressed her realization of "how my child's **brain** works, how it develops ... that their **brain** is like a radio changing stations."

ACTIVITY 12: BUILDING A BRIDGE

ACTIVITY: The object of this tactile activity is to engage parents in building a bridge in the middle of the tables out of whatever creative materials are available in their materials box. The purpose is to draw inferences between thinking and the bridge to learning.

A second purpose is built into the process of questioning strategies and how to **mediate** children to learn from the activities, how to relate what they learn to the past, and then how to transfer it to their future learning.

An emphasis is placed on bridging ideas at home to school and ideas learned in school to home.

Using wooden ice cream sticks, colored markers, crayons, glue, clay, and other craft items, participants work in teams to construct a bridge.

Decisions are made as a team regarding the rules about making, assembling, and presenting their bridge to the whole group.

BRAIN ACTIVITY: This activity requires the use of the prefrontal lobe that helps them plan for and organize the bridge construction. The dendrites fire and connect to the parietal and occipital lobes, where both spatial and visual relationship helps in the building of the bridge.

The connection of the task is then relayed to the mid**brain**, where the auditory and visual information is broken down. Participants use the hind**brain** in order to control their muscle function and coordination in handling small pieces to effect their vision of the bridge.

INSIGHTS: One parent commented, "I like a lot the construction of the bridge. To me, the construction symbolizes the construction that we as mothers build, organize, and help our kids to reach their goals."

ACTIVITY 13: STORY CUBES

ACTIVITY: Parents become adept at rolling dice that have pictures on each facet. Once the dice are rolled, parents formulate words (nouns, action words, places) to go with the pictures and create a set of sentences to make a story.

The intention of this activity is to engage parents in the simplicity of true literacy: pictures to words in literacy, making a strategic decision in how to form sentences from words, how to use imagination in the development of words to phrases, and phrases to sentences.

BRAIN ACTIVITY: Parents use their frontal lobe and connect dendrites to the occipital lobe, where their thoughts are synthesized and the process of forming the pictures on the dice into a thought pattern is made.

The interconnection then goes to the temporal lobe, where the structure and restructure of words and information take place. At this step, the interconnection of ideas to the Broca area of the **brain** occurs as a searching of words occurs. All concepts and words are stored in this area.

INSIGHTS: The story cubes activity brought a creative and interactive dynamic to the teams as stories were generated. Parents were affected notably by this activity and strategy. One participant declared, "I did not realize that learning was this easy."

ACTIVITY 14: THINK-WORD™ CARD ABCs

ACTIVITY: The purpose of this activity is to help participants learn new and efficient ways of developing **memory** and thinking with the 24 main words of the literacy part of the training program. Participants sort and organize Think-Word™ cards, then place them into a word bank on the table.

Each card is read out loud, and each definition is discussed as to its meaning. Participants then place all 24 words into ABC order.

BRAIN ACTIVITY: This activity is tactile, auditory, and visual in nature. It requires the use of the frontal lobe for planning and interconnection with the occipital lobe for processing visual information.

The connection is also made with the parietal lobe and its ability to synthesize information with the body. This process is followed by the hippocampus connecting as it collects recently received information and turns the short-term information into long-term information.

INSIGHTS: This activity was helpful in learning words in ABC order and for practicing ABC order with words starting with the same letters. Parents saw the value of this game very clearly as evidenced by the video sent from one parent participant showing how her child practiced his spelling words using the same game format.

ACTIVITY 15: WORD STRATEGY AND DICTIONARY.COM

ACTIVITY: Participants practice finding words using content concepts on blue theme cards containing words such as dinosaur or animal. They then write the word in the Thinkframes organizer and locate the meaning on Google by finding and using Dictionary.com.

Teams discuss the meaning, list what it was like, make a picture of what the content concept is, and then make a picture of what it was not. The purpose of this activity is to practice multiple steps, or **scaffold**s, of word development and comprehension building.

BRAIN ACTIVITY: The use of the frontal lobe for planning is connected to the temporal lobe for storing information. In this activity, the **brain** interconnects with the Broca and Wernicke areas of the **brain** for concept identification and concept meaning.

INSIGHTS: Parent comments emphasized the term *organization*. "If I have organization ... my child can learn," said one parent. "If I use the definition graph, and be patient and organized, my child can learn," commented another.

ACTIVITY 16: STATE ROAD MAP

ACTIVITY: Parents form teams of threes and fours. Each team receives a state map and red- and green-colored dots. The facilitator identifies a specific location on the map to begin and participants place a green dot on that location to mark where their journey begins.

The facilitator names another location on a different part of the map. The participants place a red dot there. The teams are then instructed to find three roads that would lead them on a road trip to the end.

The purpose of the activity is to demonstrate in a very tactile, visual, and kinesthetic way that the **brain** has different ways of sorting, resorting, organizing, and evaluating information to come to conclusions.

BRAIN ACTIVITY: The activity requires the use of the frontal lobe for direct thinking, **scaffold**ing, and planning for the future (or looking ahead), and for problem solving. The parietal lobe takes information in to synthesize the information spatially to physical self, processes it to distance, and draws upon the prefrontal cortex for conclusions.

INSIGHTS: One parent drew the correlation of seeing that, although there are many ways to arrive at a solution, there is usually a best way to go. She commented, "Also [we discovered] the different path[s] to solve a problem, but we need to focus on the one that is shorter or more direct [to solve the problem]."

*The learning journey begins with thinking, **scaffold**ing, planning, and problem solving.*

ACTIVITY 17: KAHOOT-IT AND MINDMEISTER

ACTIVITY: Participants use technology (iPads and smartphones) to respond to four or five survey questions posted on the Kahoot-it screen that offers two responses. Responses are submitted via a connection with Wi-Fi set up for participants.

BRAIN ACTIVITY: The participants work in teams, responding to timed question-and-answer activities. Although researchers support the idea that multitasking is not plausible for the human **brain**, this particular activity requires several **scaffold** steps of thinking, moving information from the prefrontal cortex to the occipital lobe.

In this activity, the answer is not as important as the process and procedure, which not only requires the thalamus, but also the hippocampus.

INSIGHTS: Of the 25 parents who brought an electronic device to the training, most were competent in its use and in the procedure for using an app. Parents demonstrated a lot of enthusiasm to be included in a training that used information discovery and feedback.

ACTIVITY 18: MAKE A MENU

ACTIVITY: After a **brain** mini-lecture about health and nutrition (foods to eat, foods to avoid) for children and adults, participants work together in teams to come up with a healthy menu to help the **brain** grow and develop. The purpose of this activity is to help parents understand that one of the greatest strategies they could use is their selection of food for their family.

BRAIN ACTIVITY: The Make-a-Menu activity requires the use of the prefrontal cortex to think and plan.

INSIGHTS: Parents expressed ideas about food and the selection of "healthy is better." Comments included, "[I learned that it is important] to eat healthier," to "drink more water than Coke." "[I learned that it is important] to eat healthy." "[I learned that the development] of the children's stages of the **brain** are important."

*The author (back row, center) surrounded by the mommies, all wearing **brain** hats (Activity 2).*

We did it! (State Road Map, Activity 16)

Section IV
Measuring the Efficacy of Your Training Program

CHAPTER 17
Evaluation

I have been an educator my entire adult life, and many of the members on my contributing team have advanced degrees in education. In order to succeed in the field of my passion, I have added and integrated what seems to be the equivalent of another degree: that of educational evaluation.

As a teacher, it is easy to evaluate an individual student or relate a success story from a parent who participated in a training program. The granular level is definitely easier to talk about, but that is not how our programs are considered by outside entities, such as school boards and government agencies responsible for program funding.

Evaluation is not just best practice; it is part of a fiduciary responsibility.

Whenever the paperwork or bureaucracy becomes a challenge, I remind myself that the word *value* is embedded right there inside *evaluation* (the Latin root word is *valere*, meaning strength, wellness, and worth).

Evaluation is my ticket to the parade. On some days, it is a good idea to precede the curriculum, the **choreography**, the observations, and conversation to dedicate my full attention to program evaluation.

Evaluation is not always a flexible tool. I can tell a simple story in summary and let the Lickert scales speak with the numbers. Or, I can delve into a complex quantitative analysis to help administrators continue their support.

Evaluation tells the larger story. Evaluation is the book and my program is just one chapter. Here are some questions to ask yourself as you think about evaluation:

- Is there continuity and flow in my program?
- Does my program fit seamlessly into the district, state, and federal narrative?
- Does my program align with needs and standards?
- Was my program effective?
- Were there any parts that were ineffective? If so, what can I do to change them?
- What evidence do I have that it was?
- Did I have a beginning benchmark so I can see the dramatic areas of improvement, and those areas where progress was limited?
- Did I test at the appropriate intervals so I know whether the program is on track?
- Perhaps my parents all returned for Day Two, but are they learning with the same intensity they did on Day One when everything was novel and interesting?
- Do I have a mechanism where my feedback loop can help modify or adjust my program, including communication with my facilitators? Are they flexible

enough to incorporate the feedback, or are they like a train heading down a track without any change in course?

- Are my **evaluation methods** as diverse as they need to be? Do I mix surveys (quantitative) with interviews (qualitative) to enhance my understanding?

A SKILL SET FOR THE FUTURE

As we move toward the future and stand in front of parents to speak of the compelling need for lifelong learning, program coordinators and administrators need to master the skills of evaluation through professional development.

Evaluation is a difficult skill that educators and those serving the school community need to understand. The skill of understanding data can help coordinators explain the growth, progress, and the effectiveness of a program.

CHAPTER 18
Training Feedback Tools

Feedback is the breakfast of champions.

— Ken Blanchard

PRETRAINING INSIGHTS

For my training with parents in Texas, I supplemented the simple three-question Parent Orientation Survey with a more extensive eight-question Pretraining Questionnaire (See Appendix), given to participants at lunchtime on the first day of the training.

I wanted this questionnaire to help me understand, in more detail, the demographics and the neighborhoods where the parents lived. I wanted to understand their backgrounds and education history. I received primary research data that supported the efficacy of our program within the community. The data also provided solid evidence that **brain-based** training is valuable in transitioning parents to become committed stakeholders in the school community.

FEEDBACK LOOP

Responses to the questionnaire revealed that we had attracted an equal number of parent participants from both of the schools. This meant our marketing goals had been achieved.

The majority of parents responded that they felt confused, found it difficult, or did not know how to help with family organization, much less homework. That gave us something to emphasize in this and future trainings: homework.

A small number of participants did not complete the survey. It was possible that they did not understand the questions or were reluctant to admit they could not read.

This reminded me to be on the lookout for anyone expressing confusion over meeting a task. We have to present information so that they understand and it is clear to them. Rephrasing or demonstrating using signs and hand gestures often helps.

The response phrase "try to help" appeared frequently, which told me the parents desperately wanted help. I had a motivated group; apathy would not be a problem.

An overwhelming number of the parents indicated that they had no information about their child's **brain** or how it works in the learning process. I used this information to design my **Brain** b.i.t.s.™ as simple and fun, dependent on visuals rather than words to aid learning.

Very few of these responses surprised me based on my experience and knowledge of this community and others I had serviced. Informed by the data and insight culled directly from participants, I was ready to share it with my trainers and proceed with the training.

DAY ONE KICKOFF QUESTIONS

We began with just three questions, in English and Spanish, on a single page for simplicity. The questions were completed the very first morning of the training.

1. What was school like for me?
2. What do I want school to be like for my children?
3. As a parent, what role do I want to play in my children's school environment and learning process?

My facilitators shared the thoughts from the parents during times of activities and mini-lectures or talks. There was no need to entice the parents to share their thoughts; they were encouraged to speak freely and ask questions.

The participants expressed that they liked school to varying degrees. They noted that, for them, school meant learning the basic subjects without all the testing that their children now undergo in American schools. Words such as *stress, stressful,* and *exams* caused some parents to express a belief that schools were becoming harmful to their children's health.

In terms of what they wanted from schools for their children, the participants cited less stress, more reading, and more of an understanding about the academic work their children need to complete, especially homework.

It was clear that participants felt an obligation to work with their children at home. Many of the participants expressed difficulty in knowing how to assist their children with homework. "I try to help him so he knows what he has to do," said one participant.

"I look for someone who can explain the assignment to me so I can help," said another. This confirmed the homework issue identified in the original pre-training questionnaires. We were right on track.

FOCUS GROUP FINDINGS

At the conclusion of training on the third day, the participants were divided into two focus groups on a volunteer basis.

This allowed me to see how they bonded, built on social capital, and had similar thoughts, feelings, and shared beliefs.

We limited the focus group to six participants, small enough to share thoughts, yet large enough to collect a wide range of diverse thinking.

The focus group discussions generated ideas, beliefs, and opinions that might not have been revealed in individual interviews.

The questions were presented to the participants in both English and Spanish. We used reflective questioning strategies that were captured on video.

Following the training, we translated and transcribed the video-recorded answers for the purpose of describing how the training helped the participants individually and as a group.

Structured Focus Group Questions (English)

1. What are your thoughts and opinions about this training?
2. What are your feelings about what you learned? How will it help you?
3. What are your thoughts and predictions about how this training can help you, your children, and your family?

4. What were your expectations for this training?
5. How do you expect to use these ideas?
6. How are the ideas that you have been learning different from your involvement with school previously?
7. Do you think your relationship with your children will grow and change? If so, how?
8. Do you think your connection to the school will change, and if so, how?
9. How can you take what you have learned and make it last a long time?
10. How will you help your children with their homework now?

What We Learned from the Focus Groups

During the focus group, parents discussed the changing relationships with their children, their feeling of connection to the school, what they learned, how to extend it to their home environment to support academic learning, and their new skills in helping their children with their homework.

I studied the transcriptions further and identified four common elements that Hispanic parents felt were barriers to their connections with their children's schools. They were:

1. Homework assistance
2. The importance of relationships with their children
3. Their role and relationship to school and teachers
4. The importance of social capital building, responsibility, and teamwork

I now had end-to-end and rigorous documentation directly from my parents. It allowed me to summarize my program benefits to my **parent engagement** coordinator and the school administrators.

We also had a benchmark for future programs.

CHAPTER 19
Conclusion

Education is not a tool for development — individual, community and the nation. It is the foundation for our future. It is empowerment to make choices and emboldens the youth to chase their dreams.

— Nita Ambani, The Reliance Foundation

Thank you for completing the journey of reading my book. *¡Andamio!* is grounded in the research and experience distilled from my dissertation from Nova Southeastern University, and the many years of building the engagement **model** that enhanced my reflections on the pragmatic and specific needs of school district coordinators.

My hope is that this copy of *¡Andamio!* will remain in a prominent place on your desk or bookshelf, and that it will be dog-eared, highlighted, and marked on multiple pages. I believe you will find the Appendix that follows especially helpful. There is even a reading list if you want to dive deeper and expand your horizons.

You are not in this alone. Cultivating the support of school principals, parent liaisons, and parent volunteers will give you solid footing for reaching out to parents. The process and experience of planning and implementing parent-engagement training will give you incredible confidence going forward. You will have up to 40 new parent allies after a successful program.

Those parents will become a reservoir for you in the future. They will help you recruit the next round of parents, and one or two might have the interest or potential to move into a parent training coach role. Who knows?

I cannot overemphasize the power of listening. If we can encourage parents to listen to their children about their daily lives and studies, and we then listen to the parents with their challenges and breakthroughs, I see this as the ultimate in achieving success.

Brain-based learning, at its core, supports the concept of listening and observing with our other senses, and then making improvements in the learning pathways of children, schools, and entire **communities**.

As parents and students, as coordinators and educators, each of us has 100 billion **brain** cells (and an equal number of neurons) at our disposal just waiting to take us there. I believe with all my heart and with all my experience and research, that this is the way forward.

Class dismissed!

AFTERWORD

If the technology platform for society can now turn over in five to seven years, but it takes ten to fifteen years to adapt to it ... we will all feel out of control, because we can't adapt to the world as fast as it is changing. By the time we get used to the change, that won't even be the prevailing change anymore—we will be onto some new change.

— Thomas Friedman

Just after the first publication and launch of *¡Andamio!* transpired, myriad changes specifically due to the COVID-19 pandemic occurred in our schools, sending us indoors for months. The decision to move face-to-face K-12 learning to online and distance learning emerged within a 24-hour timeframe, and educators scrambled to transition to distance learning and online teaching within a mere few days. The sheer whiplash of this rapid change to home-based learning brought a whole new set of unintended issues for **communities** of teachers and parents, including a new set of school-to-home **barriers**.

Barriers include any number of social, community, public health, family, and school issues, and includes communication between teachers and parents, and purposeful engagement programs and training for **communities** of parents.

How American schools adapted to the massive change for all stakeholders became one of the most scrutinized topics in the public politic. Therefore, this Afterword offers a brief synopsis of some—but more likely not all—of the effects of the new barriers exacerbated by the school shutdowns.

According to *Common Sense Media*, in 2020, approximately 15 to 16 million K-12 students were living in homes with no Internet connection. It was the lack of connectivity with the school and classroom that brought to light the new issues. The continuous questions from parents seeking to connect to the learning platforms emerged as a leading barrier.

Barriers Highlighted by the COVID-19 Pandemic

Barriers are obstacles to building social capital in school **communities** for the purpose of increasing collaborations and partnerships in academic growth for ELL children. Pre-pandemic, barriers—perceived or real—applied inequitably to Hispanic parents and their role in the social impact and social contract with their child's education. After the pandemic hit, the question of how to continue to educate America's children translated to how children's **brain** would adapt to the shift in learning completely online and how to continue to engage with both students and parents in that new process.

The vital challenge for today's parents is owning a device that can handle up-to-date software programs and knowing how to use both the software and the device. In the absence of these two factors, these are the homes that will have children with the greatest learning loss.

How will school districts and states implement new and innovative strategies to help these parents accommodate the growth and pace of change? As noted by David Eagleman, what will be the result of the **brain**'s plasticity when children are learning completely online? How will they adjust to the changes, as noted by Freidman, without the socio-emotional system of connected pieces of cognition and the work of the limbic system that engages both students and parents? Eagleman noted that in order to become "invested, curious, and interested" in what and how children and parents learn is to make their **brains** become more actively **engaged**.

Children's **brains** have adapted easily to the new way of learning, much more quickly than their parents. Parents must learn to trust in the ability of their children to accomplish the learning tasks presented to them in distance learning, which requires early online parent training. Following the same **model** as face-to-face parent training outlined in this book, here are a few helpful suggestions to follow for online parent training.

1. Survey the parents. Find out what you can leverage from student home lives to spark learning.
2. Build and cultivate parent learning **communities** through systematic marketing for the purpose of building an online community.
3. Train parents early in the school year. Give parents incentives to become involved.
4. Run rolling sessions of training for parents and offer some type of reward.
5. Give parents a sense of control by providing guidelines.
6. Use digital learning strategies and activities to increase more engagement and participation.

7. Train parents in critical home routines and learning for their children.

The pandemic turned several key issues into more serious barriers. They include the following: the increased barrier of food insecurity for children learning at home due to reliance on meals at school; the lack of community sharing and shelter that schools normally provide; an increase in homeless children and families; the lack of supervision at home while one or both parents are working; parents who are unable or unwilling to "sign on" to daily teacher lessons. Consider having no access to electricity or Internet connection.

Parents and administrators, as well as teachers, are now questioning how the old system of face-to-face learning will merge with the new system of distance learning. Who will be able to lead the way for a more innovative, compelling sense of teaching and learning?

Two insightful thought leaders in this issue of change, both David Eagleman and Justin Reich connect the **brain**'s ability to grow with learning in a world of technology. Eagleman reminded us through his exploration of the **brain** and ability to grow that every child living now has a **brain** that developed as part of the *Swipe Generation.*

The swift-but-necessary process to transition from face-to-face learning to online teaching in K-12 classrooms across the country affected not just millions of K-12 students but one or more of their parents. Across the country, parents suddenly had to meet the educational needs of their children by assisting them with online learning. Teaching strategies that included kinesthetic and tactile learning processes, grouping, socio-emotional learning, and moving about became limited tools for teachers. No matter how competent, teachers did not know how to continue the learning processes for children that occur through face-to-face interactivity, such as developing socio-emotional skills, playing with peers, developing relationships with peers, learning games or blocks, etc. As Reich noted, many teachers, regardless of their best efforts to transition to online learning, realized all too quickly that there were greater challenges than the role technology previously played in a classroom.

APPENDIX
Key Terms

Academic Achievement or Academic Success for ELLs

According to a review of the Language Instruction Educational Program by Faulkner-Bond et al. (2012), the Elementary and Secondary Act (ESEA) of 1965, reauthorized as NCLB (2001), provides that Title III's first purpose is to ensure that children who are limited English proficient, including immigrant children and youth, attain English proficiency, develop high levels of academic attainment in English, and meet the same challenging state academic content and student academic achievement standards all children are expected to meet.

Barriers

Barriers are obstacles to building social capital in school **communities** for the purpose of increasing opportunities and academic success for ELL children. Barriers—perceived or real—apply to Hispanic parents and their lack of involvement and/or engagement and their social impact on their child's education.

Barriers include any number of societal, community, familial, and personal issues, and lack of education, language, communication between teachers and parents, and purposeful engagement programs and training.

Brain-Based Parent Engagement Program

This term signifies a **brain-based** training program for parents in how to coach their children to think, read, write, and learn. This program develops parents' coaching skills to help their children become better critical thinkers and help parents leverage their efforts with homework, projects, questioning strategies, and strategies that bridge school learning to home learning.

Brain-Based Training

A structured, hands-on, constructivist and fully **engaged**, experience-based format in which parents of ELLs learn the principles of thinking and learning. **Brain-based** learning is an intentional form of teaching and learning using the critical parts of the **brain** most operational for the greatest amount of attention, comprehension, meaning, and **memory** factors.

Choreography

A term based on two Greek root words meaning "to write the dance." I adapted my parent program into a highly-detailed **Choreography** of Activities document that I shared with my trainers and participating parents in a workbook as a way to communicate the schedule and myriad details involved in a four-day parent training.

Collaboration

A relationship built between two or more entities with goals, missions, objectives, and activities that create a framework for potential thinking and learning success.

Constructivism

This term refers to how learners actively construct or make new knowledge based on their knowledge and understanding of prior experiences. It is based on a theory of building and internalizing new knowledge (Olivares, 2002). In this book, constructivism signifies the **scaffold**ing, or building upon prior experiences and knowledge to create new concepts and ideas.

Engagement

For the purpose of my research, engagement is "the act or state of being involved with something" (Merriam-Webster Dictionary, 2014). According to David Eagleman, the highest level of engagement occurs when the learner is "invested, curious, and interested." These three prerequisites stimulate and motivate specific parts of the **brain** to become **engaged**.

English Language Learners (ELLs)

This term applies to children who are born in the United States of first-generation immigrants, or children born in other countries who have immigrated to the United States and lack English language skills to operate functionally in the academics of American schools.

Equity

In an educational context, equity is a measure of achievement, fairness, and opportunity. Equity depends on two factors: fairness and inclusion. Fairness is present when factors specific to a student's personal conditions do not interfere with potential of academic success. Inclusion refers to a comprehensive standard that applies to everyone in an educational system.

Mediated Learning Experience (MLE)

Mediated learning experience is the intentional processing of procedures, information, and the output of thinking that must be processed in order to function in the world. Supported by Vygotsky (1978) and developed by Feuerstein, et al. (2010), mediation stresses the communal understanding of knowledge, collaborative sharing of experience, and the sorting or categorizing of ideas. The mediator helps the learner frame, filter, and schedule stimuli, and ultimately influences the potential ways that transfer of knowledge occurs in the student's thinking. Mediation assumes that instruction is more concerned with going beyond the information given by connecting the present to both the past and the anticipation of the future than with mastering specific bits of here and now data.

Parent Engagement

Parent engagement is a three-step active engagement of parents of ELLs in a structured program or training that seeks to connect and bridge the strategies for learning from school to home in a sustainable way. By way of active engagement, parents are trained and attend with continuity, learn and practice knowledge, and become competent in the process skills of thinking, reading, and writing, and finally become coaches in their children's classrooms and at home. Parents are coached to use tools to help children develop **memory** and to understand the relationships between learning a task, thinking about and creating an outcome, and building tasks one upon another, or **scaffold**ing (Cook-Cottone, 2004; Feuerstein et al., 2010).

Parent Involvement

Parent involvement is the involvement parents or legal guardians of ELLs demonstrate by seeking a connection to a fundamental role in their child's school and how it operates, what needs are addressed and provided for, what functions are available, the teachers with whom they will communicate, and the support systems the parents will work within.

Purpose

Hurst (2014) likened process and purpose when it comes to the development of an interconnected networking of relationships. Hurst noted, "The magic number was three: People gain purpose when they grow personally, when they establish meaningful relationships, and when they are in service to something greater than themselves" (p. 4). Purpose then, as it relates to this book, is connected to the role of parents and their children, school and their children, and the community.

Social Capital Building

In my research and trainings, social capital building is applied to the stakeholders in a school community. Citing Bordieu (1977, 1986), Coleman (1988), and Fitts and McClure (2015) defined social capital as "…the knowledge, resources, or other benefits that an individual can access by her social relationships and as a result of social interactions with others" (p. 295).

Coordinator Resources: Sample Surveys

Please use the questions that follow on the next three pages as the basis for creating forms to use before, during, and after **parent engagement** training.

It is hoped that you are able to adapt these questions into your own custom form on school or district letterhead and translate them into appropriate languages for your school community.

There are three templates provided are:

- Pretraining Questionnaire
- After-Training Evaluation
- Structured Focus Group Questions

PRETRAINING QUESTIONAIRE

1. What school does your child attend?

2. In what grades are your child(ren) (check all appropriate answers)

    ___ Kindergarten

    ___ First

    ___ Second

    ___ Third

    ___ Fourth

3. How do you feel about working on homework with your children?

    ___ Confused

    ___ It's Difficult

    ___ Don't Know How to Help

    ___ OK

4. Have you ever participated in a parent training where you learned how to specifically work with children to help them at school? If yes, what kind of training? If no, why not?

5. What do you do at home to help your child with his/her homework?

6. Do you know any information about your child's **brain** and how it works in the learning process?

AFTER-TRAINING EVALUATION

1. List some of the things you learned and/or liked about the training.
2. List any changes you have made at your house to help your children with schoolwork.
3. List some ways this training will help you and your family.

Please answer Yes or No to the following questions:

4. Homework time has changed at my house due to participation in this program. (___Yes ___No)
5. I feel more equipped to help my child(ren) with homework and projects. (___Yes ___No)
6. I feel more connected to the school. (___Yes ___No)
7. I feel more confident to communicate with my child(ren)'s teacher if I have questions or concerns. (___Yes ___No)

STRUCTURED FOCUS GROUP QUESTIONS

1. What are your opinions about this training?
2. What are your feelings?
3. What are your thoughts and predictions about how this training can help you and your children?
4. What were your expectations for this training?
5. How do you expect to use these ideas?
6. How are the ideas that you have been learning different from your involvement with school previously?
7. Do you think your relationship with your children will grow and change?
8. How do you think your connection to school will change?
9. How can you take what you have learned and make it last a long time?
10. How will you help your children with their homework now?

Sample Program RFP: Northeast U.S. School District

District funders and Title I Coordinators:

It is often challenging to envision the next step in building out a Title I Program. The following pages outline a sample grant proposal from a program in the Northeast U.S. that might serve as a **model** for you.

PHILOSOPHY STATEMENT AND BUSINESS FOCUS

VISION: We will ensure that all children will be critical and creative thinkers, readers and writers.

MISSION: Our mission is to promote and create school improvement and academic achievement through professional development training for teachers that leads to family engagement with parents and children for the best practices of thinking and learning. We will utilize innovative partnerships with low performing schools, the **communities** in which they exist, and the families of those students to develop students who are critical and creative thinkers, readers, and writers.

PHILOSOPHY: We believe all children can think critically and creatively in any language. According to demographers, the Hispanic population will grow to more than 41 million in the United States by 2012.

Our bilingual programs will help to serve these **communities** of children and their families.

We believe that all children, including ELL and at-risk populations, are growing up in an unprecedented information age that requires them to become more self-directed and better thinkers in the future. Faxes, Wii, X-Boxes, computers, blogs, Facebook, Twitter, social networks and sophisticated cable TV bring new information faster than it can be processed.

It's not so much that children need to absorb more information; rather, they need to be able to sort, process, and understand it better by making use of the **brain**'s ability to connect disparate elements.

We believe that the **brain** is built for thinking, learning, and digesting information. Our job is not just to feed the mind but also to help it digest and think more efficiently.

We need to build on the natural features of how the **brain** sorts, organizes, analyzes, and evaluates information in any language. All of our programs and services are built upon this philosophy.

RATIONALE: With the constantly changing face of education — new federal mandates, textbooks and technology, changing funding streams, eligibility requirements, student demographics, and fluid administrations — the Think and Learn Reform **Model** was originally designed and replicated to facilitate self-renewal and positive change management for all stakeholders.

The thinking and learning strategies and best practices used in the **model** focus on how to learn, not what to learn. This focus becomes a highly effective and results-driven **model** program with all students, and most specifically, with English Language Learners and their families.

All of the parent, teacher, and children's programs have been tested in low-performing schools with language minority/Hispanic and African-American students with outstanding results. The systemic process **model** of thinking and learning, when implemented in conjunction with positive behavioral management and learning environments, facilitates the connection among the school infrastructures, family engagement, and community involvement.

This bridging results in more focused productivity for each and every child and their family, and reduces barriers to academic success.

Through our specific programs for children, training for parents and professional development designed for teachers, Let's Think-kids Foundation, Inc., has developed a true reform **model** that ultimately leads to student success.

In response to this RFP, we are addressing the Parent/Caregiver portion of the diagram on the previous page. Parents provide the foundation for the children of today and the workers of tomorrow.

With a fluctuating economy, hectic schedules, and limited time, today's busy parents need more help and more tools to stay connected with their children and their learning at school. Parents need more tangible ways to help their children think and learn more efficiently than ever.

They need information about their children's **brains** and how they work. They need to know how nutrition affects their children's thinking and learning. They need help with strategies for homework and how to prepare their children for their future.

Let's Think-kids Foundation, Inc. offers parent programs that mirror staff development training and current teaching methods that provide consistency for students. Program methods develop and improve a parent's own coaching strategies and skills to help their children become better thinkers.

Once parents learn how to coach their children in learning how to think, the possibilities are endless. Toward that goal, we offer two programs: Think-parents are powerful™ and the Let's Think-Kids homeworkhelper mathpac™. These powerful training programs help parents leverage their efforts with homework, questioning, literacy and reading, and teach strategies that bridge school to home.

Our one-of-a-kind training is a perfect introduction for parents in:

- How their child's **brain** works at each stage of development;
- What foods are most important for thinking and learning;
- How to focus and **mediate** their child's thinking process;
- How to use strategies that help their child sort, re-sort, organize, analyze, and evaluate information;
- Practical coaching strategies to guide children through planning and finishing projects;
- Practical coaching tips in literacy and math thinking;
- Tips on how to be an efficient homework helper.

OBJECTIVE: Through our Think-parents are powerful™ program we will work in partnership with the district to provide parents of students with training, tools, and strategies to help their children become better thinkers, learners, and creative problem-solvers, as well as contributing members of the community.

APPROACH: The Let's Think-Kids Foundation, Inc. will implement its proven approach to achieve the objective.

Our approach will:

A. Focus on Parents

The Foundation's systematic process helps parents learn how to set goals for better literacy, to provide better support to their children, and then measure progress over time. This active-learning cycle has achieved the following results:

Measurable increased levels of knowledge and skills about their child's literacy learning development, and increased application of practical researched-based strategies.

B. Enhance Students' Critical Thinking Skills

The Foundation's comprehensive process helps students develop better thinking and learning strategies by integrating the support of the school system and parent **communities**. This integrated approach has achieved the following results:

1. Increased comprehension level in reading by 20%; and
2. Increased capacity to plan, think, research, and write projects.

C. Complement Existing Initiatives

The Foundation's strategies, skills, and programs work synergistically with current and future programs. The bonds created among parents, students, and educators prepare the student for more creative, robust, and **engaged** participation in other educational initiatives.

D. Focus on the Unique Needs of the Community

The first step in the Foundation's process is to assess the specific needs of the local community and configure its successful programs in a way that will work best with the local student population as well as local teachers, support staff, administrators, and resources.

SUMMARY OF RELEVANT EXPERIENCES

Let's Think-Kids Foundation, Inc. (LTKF) is the 21st-century solution to real school reform. It was originally designed as a school reform **model** for bilingual and at-risk programs under the entity of The National Children's Educational Reform Foundation, Inc. (NCERF).

LTKF is a re-formation of NCERF and holds the proprietary rights to all of the researched and highly successful programs including Thinkparents Entrepreneurs™, Thinkparents homeworkhelper™, Thinkparents are powerful™, Thinkcoach leadership academy™, Thinkcampreneur (an entrepreneur's camp for kids)™, Let'sThinkwrite™ and ThinkidsToWork™.

Let's Think-Kids Foundation, Inc. was incorporated in 2010. Its philosophy, programs, products, and services are all firmly rooted in Dr. Susan F. Tierno's original, highly developed, well-research work with NCERF.

Dr. Tierno began this journey in 1989 as Creative Thinkers, Inc., an S-Corporation in Connecticut. As its president and creative mind, she began with Seminars for Kids, a summer tutoring program. She then went on to develop corporate training, corporate consulting, and school consulting in locations including Tucson Unified, Providence, RI, public schools, Hartford, CT, public schools, and Stamford, CT, public schools.

With the help of a grants writer in the spring of 1995, Dr. Tierno joined with Hartford public schools and its bilingual department to create a $3 million federally funded partnership grant.

By August 1995, the grant awarded and Dr. Tierno founded NCERF, a 501c3 corporation located in Connecticut. To fund the programs, products, and services for school contracts, a license was designed between Creative Thinkers, Inc. and the Foundation.

The innovative **model** of cognitive programs for teachers, children, and parents was funded under federal contracts, winning more than $3.2 million during a 10-year period.

This process was implemented by licensing royalty-free to the Foundation in return for the position of director and CEO of NCERF. Creative Thinkers remained its partner in holding the trademark registrations for corporate and trade development, and licensed the trade dress and registrations of trademarked registered products and programs to the Foundation for school contracts.

The principal mission or business of the 501c3 was the design and implementation of innovative school partnerships in collaboration with bilingual education in three urban centers in the United States. This effort used a highly driven business management **model** for comprehensive school reform.

The **model** was based on a systematic process of professional development training using proprietary integrated programs with a results-driven, research-based approach. Tested process thinking and learning strategies for teachers, parents, and their children were incorporated.

The programs were specifically piloted and researched in public school systems in Hartford, CT; Dallas, Texas; and Washington, D.C.

The intentional instructional system designed by Dr. Tierno demonstrated an increase in student achievement scores, most specifically in the area of reading comprehension, via 10 years of implementation and application of thinking processes through a systematic five-step **model**.

Model steps included thinking, criteria-building, decision-making, and problem-solving skills for literacy and math for all ages, grade levels, and all academic disciplines.

According to teachers and parents of the children in their classrooms who have participated in the Think & Learn Partnerships, the program transformed at-risk students into effective, active thinkers and learners. Positive and productive classroom project outcomes of the Think & Learn/Think-kids™ program included:

- Students were more **engaged**, self-directed, independent thinkers and learners;
- Students were curious and eager to conduct investigations on their own about themes through research;
- Students as young as kindergarteners were motivated and learned to use time on task;
- Students had more control over their thinking and learning process, they were empowered with intentional bridging and questioning processes;
- Students created cohesive teams and a sense of classroom community;

- Less time was wasted on behavioral problems. Teachers had more time for individual and team Think-coaching;
- Students felt confident with the planning and organizational process of the curriculum;
- Teachers felt excited about teaching results and the impact that they were making on the students;
- Teachers saw improved literacy and numeracy, as well as problem solving in math. Scores demonstrated as much as 25% higher on standardized tests;
- Children demonstrated a more project-directed manner of thinking and, in turn, improved their reading for information and their writing skills by 18 to 20% increases in comprehension.

In 2005, Dr. Tierno began preparing her programs for national implementation in response to No Child Left Behind and its failed efforts toward improving academic achievement of English Language Learners.

She moved to Maryland to avail herself of opportunities in Washington, D.C., where she **engaged** in important dialogue and associations with leading educators and lawmakers to determine how her programs would best fit the changing education needs of the nation.

For the last several years, Dr. Tierno has worked diligently to research, adjust, enhance, and expand her best practices curriculum with the benefit of input from graduate students, new teachers, and practitioners. She is ready to continue the important work of helping to prepare our students and their families for the future.

SCOPE OF SERVICES

Let's Think-kids Foundation, Inc. is a national education nonprofit organization focused on serving English Language Learners and at-risk minority youth and their families. Through partnerships with schools and school districts, our goal is to improve academic achievement that begins with professional development and parent training, and extends to helping students develop critical thinking skills, become creative thinkers, and excel as readers and writers.

The mission cannot be achieved in isolation. Without the engagement of families and parents / caregivers, a supportive environment that enhances feelings of confidence and self-worth within their children is difficult to maintain.

Over the past 20 years, our solutions have focused on structured programs with best practices aimed at helping parents and their children leverage and maximize their learning together to achieve at a level necessary to function efficiently and effectively in a global market economy.

The Scope of Services involves:

- Stakeholder building (parent facilitators, community volunteers, teachers, administrators, and parents of children in schools)
- Training of Trainers (parent facilitators, administrators, and teachers)
- Program Training (parent facilitators, administrators, teachers, and parents of children in schools)
- Evaluation (on project partnership)
- **Think-parents are powerful™:** A powerful training for parents in how to think, how to read and how to learn, this program develops parents' coaching skills to help their children become better thinkers. Parents

learn how to provide a supportive, encouraging at-home environment that facilitates continuity in their child's learning process. This program helps parents leverage their efforts with homework, projects, questioning strategies, and ways that bridge school to home.

Parents involved in this training will learn:

- How their children's **brain**s work at each stage of development;
- How to focus their children's thinking processes;
- How to use Think-frames™ to help their children sort and organize information;
- Practical coaching strategies and tips for mediating thinking with their children;
- Practical coaching tips in thinking and reading with their children;
- Practical tips in school and home connections.

Together with the district, a specific number of parents will be actively involved in a number (to be determined) of training sessions that will specifically meet the following three goals, as well as any other goals the stakeholders from Waterbury public schools believe would enhance parent involvement and student academic achievement.

GOAL ONE: To recruit and engage ELL and at-risk minority parents/caregivers through training and activities that refocus and fortify their role as it relates to instructional design, teaching and learning processes, and site-based operations to effect positive, measurable support and improvement in language proficiency, academic performance, and workforce readiness among their children in grades pre-K through 12.

GOAL TWO: To redesign and reframe the teaching/ learning process within bilingual and at-risk minority classrooms via implementation of leadership training and professional staff development, and facilitation of parent/ teacher collaboration to effect measurable improvement in language skills, academic performance, and workforce readiness among ELL and at-risk minority students in grades pre-K through 12.

GOAL THREE: To train parents/caregivers of the ELL student and at-risk population to become thinking coaches and advocates for their children, thereby improving the thinking and learning skills that complement and enhance existing programs that prepare them to: a) become more critical thinkers, planners, evaluators, and communicators; b) generate improved academic performance as measured by statewide standard examinations; and c) become resource-based learners to meet the needs of the 21st century workforce.

RECRUITMENT OF PARENT/CAREGIVER PARTICIPANTS

In collaboration with parent facilitators, LTKF will work with individual school personnel and community members to recruit parents/caregivers to participate in our training.

During our initial round of stakeholder meetings with the public schools, we will develop a marketing and promotional campaign specifically for this purpose.

LTKF possesses a highly specialized program for marketing and stakeholder building, which is designed to work in conjunction with an assigned director and facilitator for the project from the Waterbury schools. This marketing campaign will be built with the help of all stakeholders within the district and within the **communities**.

In order to help with the entire mission of this **parent engagement** project, it is proposed that school facilitators (parent facilitators, community volunteers, teachers, administrators, and parents of children in schools) should be the first to be trained. These facilitators will become equipped with the necessary tools to yield a high quality of interest and a high quantity of family participation to lay the groundwork for several phases of the LTKF blueprint **model**.

OUTLINE OF TRAINING PROGRAMS

OBJECTIVE: Through our Think-parents are Powerful™ program, LTKF will work in partnership with the public schools to provide parents of minority and at-risk students in Waterbury schools with training, tools, and strategies to help their children become better thinkers, learners, and creative problem-solvers, as well as contributing members of the community.

APPROACH: LTKF will implement its proven approach to achieve the objective that will:

A. Focus on Parents

The Foundation's systematic process helps parents learn how to set goals for better literacy, to provide better support to their children, and then measure progress over time. This active learning cycle has achieved the following results:

1. Increased levels of knowledge and skills about their child's literacy learning development; and
2. Increased application of practical researched-based strategies.

B. Enhance Critical Thinking Skills

The Foundation's comprehensive process helps students develop better thinking and learning strategies by integrating the support from the school system and parent **communities**. This integrated approach has achieved the following results:

1. An increased comprehension level in reading by 20%; and
2. An increased capacity to plan, think, research, and write projects.

C. Complement Existing Initiatives

The Foundation's strategies, skills, and programs work synergistically with current and future programs. The stronger bonds created among parents, student, and educators prepare the student for more creative, robust, and **engaged** participation in other educational initiatives.

D. Focus on the Unique Needs of the Community

The first step in the Foundation's process is to assess the specific needs of the local community and configure its programs in a way that will work best with the local student population as well as local teachers, support staff, and administrators.

The above goals are met through strong leadership development with teachers, parents, and stakeholders in schools.

ASSESSMENT AND EVALUATION

This section provides an explanation of how the project will measure an increase in student achievement through assessment, attendance, and behavior data. For the purpose of this description, we define behavior data to include in-school behavior required for student thinking and learning outcomes. We also will define at-home behaviors needed for student achievement.

LTKF will partner with Dr. Libia Gil, a senior fellow with the American Institute of Research, to evaluate the effectiveness of our education methods, **models**, practices, and technologies on student learning. Participants in this development project will be aligned in an evaluation project with the hypothesis that both critical and creative thinking literacy can be highly evident as aligned with content standards. Using a random sample, experimental and control groups will be selected for study participation.

The overall hypothesis or conclusion of the study will be that students and their parents who receive the highly creative cognitive-based instruction (LTKF group) will show increase in academic achievement with higher percentage scores. The theory and potentially reported practice will suggest the inherent efficacy of the best practice and the overall **model**.

Consistently, LTKF and its cognitive-based instructional programs increased student achievement through identified pilot project classrooms that targeted the needs of individual state testing requirements.

While this was beneficial to each of the districts, the differences in requirements, approaches, evaluations, and criteria over the course of 12 years made it difficult to compare results. Because of strong evidence that LTKF's programmatic practices, strategies, and programs used within the districts yielded promising results in each district, despite variables, the one common factor among all districts pointed to parent behavior and involvement.

This underscores the necessity of developing more of a **model**-based research design, in which baseline assessment, feedback, data collection, and parent participation are included in the **model**. Such a systematic plan will be designed with the district by the LTKF evaluation team.

LTKF believes that a more formal and systematic study is warranted with a clear reasonable hypothesis to inform research in such a manner that will help to improve the academic achievement in the future for ELL and special needs students, and other low-performing schools in the project, while informing the national audience of its efforts. Otherwise, important information about innovation and the **model**'s impact on school achievement will be lost.

The proposed research **model** for this grant will include a design that uses the most rigorous standards for education research and evaluation. This method will be a scientifically based research design that has the following elements:

1. Employment of systematic, empirical methods that draw on a series of experiments;

2. Involvement of rigorous data analyses that are adequate to test the stated hypotheses and justify the general conclusions drawn (in this case, student achievement and the effect of the partnership **model**);

3. Reliance on measurements that provide reliable and valid data across evaluators and observers, across multiple measurements and observations, and across studies by the same or different investigators (triangulation);

4. Use of an experimental design in which individuals, the program, and the educational activities are assigned to different conditions and with appropriate controls to evaluate the effects of the condition of interest, with focus on random-assignment experiments that contain within-condition or across-condition controls;

5. Assurance that the experimental study will be presented in sufficient detail and clarity to allow for replication; and

6. Acceptance by a peer-reviewed journal or approved by a panel of independent experts through a comparably rigorous, objective, and scientific review (What Works Clearing House is one of the goals for this project).

The **model** evaluation construction will be based on a clear hypothesis.

To that end, the hypothesis measures and analysis might look somewhat like the table below:

INPUTS Resources	Constraints: Limitations to Improvements	Activities / Services	OUTCOMES Benefits
2 principals at 2 elementary sites as stakeholders	Attendance at start-up stakeholder meeting during April	Participation and time in brief meeting about the parent research project	Stakeholder acceptance and promotion
Superintendent Executive Assistant Title 1 Parent Coordinator Federal Grant Director 2 school principals 1 vice principal 1 instructional coach	Time use in day	Input and time	Attendance and participation in upfront stakeholder meeting
Tour of the schools Dovalina McDonnell	Knowledge in how-to recruit the specific ELL parents from all grades at their school sites	To market and communicate and gain commitment from parents to attend the training	Demonstrates applicability for ALL parents of English Language learners and their children
25 parents per model site as research participants			Increase in focus, behaviors and skills

Think-parents are powerful™ coach training materials			Complete package of professional dev. materials with all the tools needed to teach program and lessons better
Professional Development Children's libraries as resources given A complete 5-step Systematic Approach and a complete project-based program	Lack of structured training programs for parents	Materials and program in two languages. ESL teachers provided in classrooms to help classroom teacher	Meets the needs of teachers and schools having Professional Development libraries and resources; meets the needs of teachers having resource materials for their students
Think-parents are powerful program™ for parents of children in each of the 2 schools. Superintendent offered: 1. The CIVIC Center; plus a room for the childcare 2. Technology department to video the days of training	Schedules and participation history	One-day orientation and explanation of the research adult consent form 4 days of parent training on the program Follow-up days for coaching support and feedback	Development of parents as coaches to help their children with thinking, reading and writing homework
Programmatic evaluation	Not enough start-up data on schools, parents and their engagement with homework and classrooms	Stakeholder meetings and questionnaire development	Potential decision-making for building capacity with the program

HYPOTHESIS

There is a relationship between the three significant stakeholders around the nexus of thinking literacy: teachers, parents, and other stakeholders.

MEASURES

Assessment data will be extracted from the following tools of measurement:

- Surveys for all stakeholders
- Lykert scales
- Las Links
- SAT 10
- Aprenda, Logramos
- Woodcock Munoz
- State standardized assessments in English and Spanish
- Data on standard demographics, graduation, retention, and absences will be collected
- Formative and summative periodic evaluation to help with monitoring and improving the project's implementation
- Context antecedent evaluation with triangulation

ANALYSIS

Analysis of collected data includes the following:

- Moment correlations
- Critical questionnaires and record reviews of stakeholders involved
- Observations of key teacher behaviors and student outcomes to inform best practices after trainings
- To examine the possibility of moderator effects: ELL vs. non-ELL, ELL control vs. non-ELL non-control

In order to determine the value of the collected data relative to other data, the following questions will be explored:

- What unique design element, administrative components, and participant characteristics affected the project's implementation, outcomes, and impact?
- Which of these elements, components, and characteristics must be in place for successful replication and sustainability?
- Were particular success or problems attributable to unique site characteristics or conditions?
- What specific aspects of each of the trainings lead to the success of student academic achievement?
- What measures were used to reach conclusions concerning effectiveness of the training and its effect on academic achievement in ELL children?

Thought Leaders:
Some Book Recommendations

People know I am an avid reader. They often ask what I am reading. Over the decades, I have grown to love many authors, for their purpose, their thoughts, their intelligence, and their focus on their writing, which keeps me, as a reader, clear about who I am. Here are just a few I would recommend:

DAVID BROOKS

The Second Mountain **(2019)**

David Brooks has become one of my favorites. He, too, has gone through change in life and writes so meaningfully about **communities** and the need for trust, communication, and mutual belongingness.

BRENEE BROWN

Daring Greatly **(2012);** *Rising Strong* **(2017);**
Dare to Lead **(2018)**

Brenee Brown is one of my all-time favorite thought leaders on the human emotion of vulnerability and courage. She not only has thoughts about our emotional exposure, but she has data to back it up. Brenee is on YouTube and now has a Netflix show.

WILLIAM CALVIN

How Brains Think (1996)

William Calvin writes such an interesting and fascinating book on the **brain** and its evolving intelligence. I thought it was going to be boring and technical, but I could not put it down. Intelligence deals with the know-how, and the know-what of the **brain**. It is all about process.

MIHALY CSIKSZENTMIHALYI

Flow: The Psychology of Optimal Experience (1990); *Creativity: Flow and the Psychology of Discovery and Invention* (1996)

Both Csikszentmihalyi books are informative as to how I, myself, think and work. His discussion about courage, resilience, perseverance, mature defense, and transformational skills are all structures of the mind that help us cope with the demands of everyday life.

DAVID EAGLEMAN

Livewired: The inside story of the ever-changing brain (2020); *Incognito: The Secret Lives of the Brain* (2011); *The Brain: The story of you* (2015)

David Eagleman is a renowned neuroscientist. He teaches and speaks on **brain** plasticity, or the changing patterns of the **brain**. The best thing about this author is not just his work, his data, and his ideas; it is the simple way he explains through stories all about how our **brains** change. I like the story of the London Cabbies the best!

THOMAS FRIEDMAN

The World is Flat (2007); *Thank You for Being Late* (2016)

Thomas Friedman has been a 30-year favorite of mine. His editorials in the *New York Times* led me to his books. His perspective settles my **brain** into accepting the change process in our society, our culture, the technology, and, specifically, in my life. His work on the coming of technology and his message about how we are really competing globally is profound. Further, his message is impactful as it relates to the growth and pace of change in technology today.

AARON HURST

The Purpose Economy: How Your Desire for Impact, Personal Growth and Community is Changing the World (2014)

Aaron Hurst has written the most meaningful book on purpose. There are three types: personal purpose, social purpose, and societal purpose. Purpose is all about how we approach our work. This book is one of my favorites. It helps me clearly understand our changes in society and the new generations, and their impact on purpose.

STEVEN JOHNSON

Farsighted: How We Make the Decisions that Matter the Most (2018)

Steven Johnson writes about decision-making. He discusses life-altering decisions and introduces the reader to powerful tools for dealing with the complexity of decision-making. One thing I have learned over my lifetime that he emphasizes: "The smartest decision-makers don't go with their guts."

DANIEL KAHNEMAN

Thinking Fast and Slow (2011)

Daniel Kahneman is a unique and, interestingly, one of our most important thinkers who **engaged** me as a reader in his description of how we think, the benefit of slowing our thinking, and where and how we can and cannot trust our intuition.

JUSTIN REICH

Failure to Disrupt: Why Technology Alone can't Transform Education (2020)

Justin Reich is a professor at MIT. His focus is education, technology, and the future of schools. He notes that technology is not the only answer. Much is needed in terms of reform and technology is not a reform improvement.

Acknowledgments

They say a mother holds your hand for a while, but your heart forever. Thank you, Ma … And to dear old Dad. You gave me wings to fly. Thanks, Pop.

Not enough can be said about great people who have entered my life at one point or another and have influenced me in one or more ways. I am lucky to have met these people:

To **Dr. Ana Maria Rodriguez:** My mentor, my sister, my life-long **role model for bright, intelligent women in this lifetime.**

To **Dr. Karen Bowser**, for her watchful eyes, her strong guidance, and her cheerleading through the doctoral program and, most specifically, the study that led to this book.

To **Pat Campos,** who had the fortitude, courage, and patience to help me through the total research-study-boots-on-the-ground process. Without you, this book would not have come to a reality.

Contributors

CAROLYN BURNS BASS
Andamio Press Webmaster

Carolyn Burns Bass is a business arts specialist who excels at providing creative solutions for the business of life. A creative writer who has published nonfiction and fiction, she uses her experience as an editor and journalist to blend words with pictures to tell stories that empower people and promote products through social media, websites, and print.

DR. KAREN BOWSER
Dissertation Chair, Nova Southeastern University

Dr. Karen Bowser, an award-winning educator, has spent her professional career developing and delivering innovative learning and educational programs in a variety of corporate, government, and academic settings.

Dr. Bowser has served as the Executive Director of Professional Development; the Dean of Professional Development and Field Services; the Associate Dean of Doctoral Studies at Abraham S. Fischler School of Education; a dissertation chair; and Program Professor of Organizational Development, Adult

Education, and Higher Education at Nova Southeastern University. In addition, Dr. Bowser served as the Director of Professional Education for a large consulting firm. She has taught at Penn State University in its education and humanities departments, and directed the learning and writing center. Throughout her career, she has taught every level from preschool through doctoral level.

PAT CAMPOS
Coordinator, Laredo Independent School District,
Laredo, Texas

Ms. Campos has been the Title I Coordinator of Parent and Family Engagement at the Laredo Independent School District since 2013. For 30 years she worked for Webb County Juvenile Youth Village and retired as the Director of Probation Services. She served close to 12 years as a school board member, three years as a school board president, and has 30 years of experience working with youth and their families through her job, the school board, Girl Scouts, and Catholic Youth Ministry. In 2018, she was appointed to serve on the Texas Council for Family/School Engagement.

LAURA A. MARSALA
Editor, Production Coordinator

Ms. Marsala has worked closely with Dr. Tierno since 1995 as an editor, copywriter, graphics designer, and brand developer. She earned a bachelor of arts degree in English/journalism from Central Connecticut State University. She has held positions as marketing project manager; art director, copy editor, and paginator at several New England newspapers; edited books on a range of topics; planned and coordinated marketing programs for nonprofits; and has more than 42 years of experience in prepress production.

JON OBERMEYER
Project Director, Editorial Content and Production

Mr. Obermeyer holds a degree in English from Westmont College and an M.F.A. in creative writing from the University of North Carolina at Greensboro. He has been a commercial loan officer, economic developer, small business owner, marketing director for a global technology consulting firm, and assistant to the publisher of the *San Francisco Chronicle*, before embarking on a "second-act" career as a freelance writer, developmental editor, and writing coach. He has published 20 books of creative work and four writing guides on Amazon, and is a three-time finalist for the James Applewhite Poetry Prize in North Carolina.

DR. ANA MARIA RODRIQUEZ
Vice Provost for Undergraduate Education (Retired),
University of Texas-Pan American and Parent Trainer

Dr. Rodriguez retired as Senior Vice Provost for Undergraduate Studies at the University of Texas Pan American. During her 46-year career in education, she taught students in secondary public schools, prepared graduate students in a university counselor education program, and served as administrator for undergraduate programs at the university level.

Her work involved serving approximately 80% Hispanic students—many of whom were English language learners—and their parents—many of whom spoke only Spanish. She encountered many students who had struggled through the public school educational systems and survived; but she also encountered many who did not.

As a result, she made it her life's work to identify the needs of these learners and their parents, plan and implement programs and strategies to meet the needs, and mentor and coach future educators. Dr. Rodriguez has conducted staff development and training programs for school boards, school district personnel, and parents in the areas of Parental Involvement, Cooperative Learning and Guidance and Counseling.

Works Cited

Front matter

Caine, R. N., & Caine, G. (1994). *Making connections: Teaching and the human brain.* Boston, MA: Addison-Wesley Longman, Inc.

Chapter 1

Brooks, D. (2019). *The second mountain: The quest for a moral life.* New York: Random House.

Caine, R. N., & Caine, G. (1996). *Making connections: Teaching and the human brain.* Boston, MA: Addison-Wesley Longman, Inc.

El Yaafouri, L. (April 30, 2019). *Identifying and supporting gifted ELLs.* Edutopia (George Lucas Educational Foundation). Retrieved from edutopia.org/article/identifying-and-supporting-gifted-ells

Friedman, T. (2017). *Thank you for being late: An optimist's guide to thriving in the age of accelerations.* New York: Farrar, Straus & Giroux.

Kamanentz, A., & Weiner, C. (2019). At your wits' end with a screen-obsessed kid? National Public Radio Life Kit Series. Retrieved from npr.org/2019/06/30/736214974/at-your-wits-end-with-a-screen-obsessed-kid-read-this

Marx, G. (2014). *Twenty-one trends for the 21st century: Out of the trenches and into the future.* Bethesda, MD: Education Week Press.

Murdock, S. H. (2012). *Population growth in the United States: Implications for education and economic development.* America's Promise, Washington, DC. Retrieved from tawb.org/wp-content/uploads/2017/03/MurdockDemoSlide2017.pdf

Reich, J. (2020). *Failure to disrupt: Why technology alone can't transform education.* Cambridge, MA: Harvard University Press.

Chapter 2

Jensen, E. P. (2005). *Teaching with the brain in mind* (2nd ed.). Thousand Oaks, CA: Corwin.

Eagleman, D. (2020) *Livewired: The inside story of the ever-changing brain.* New York, NY: Pantheon.

Quezada, M. S. (June 14, 2018). Engaging families: The power of a whole school, multi-strategy approach, in *Social Innovations Journal*. Retrieved from socialinnovationsjournal.org/editions/issue-48/116-innovative-models/2835-engaging-families-the-power-of-a-whole-school-multi-strategy-approach

Chapter 3

Brooks, D. (2019). *The second mountain: The quest for a moral life*. New York: Random House.

Jensen, E. P. (2009). *Teaching with poverty in mind*. Alexandria, VA: ASCD Books.

Chapter 4

Blankstein, A. M., & Noguera, P. (2016). *Excellence through equity: Five principles of courageous leadership to guide achievement for every student*. Alexandria, VA: ASCD Books.

Caine, R. N., & Caine, G. (1996). *Making connections: Teaching and the human brain*. Boston, MA: Addison-Wesley Longman, Inc.

Hart, L. (1983). *The human brain and human learning*. New York, NY: Longman.

Jensen, E. (2005). *Teaching with the brain in mind* (2nd ed.). Alexandria, VA: ASDC.

Sousa, D. (2005). *How the ELL brain learns to read* (2nd ed.). Thousand Oaks, CA: Corwin.

Chapter 5

Caine, R. N., & Caine, G. (1996). *Making connections: Teaching and the human brain*. Boston, MA: Addison-Wesley Longman, Inc.

Calvin, W. H. (1996). *How brains think*. New York: Basic Books.

Tierno, Susan F. (2016). *An exploration of the impact of brain-based training on Hispanic parents of English language learner elementary-age children* (Doctoral dissertation). Nova Southeastern University, Fort Lauderdale, FL.

Chapter 6

Khatchadourian, R. (Nov. 19, 2018). *Degrees of freedom: A scientist's work linking minds and machines.* Retrieved from blackrockmicro.com/degrees-of-freedom/

Chapter 7

Schacter, D. (2002). *The seven sins of memory: How the mind forgets and remembers.* Boston, MA: Houghton Mifflin.

Sousa, D. (2017). *How the ELL brain learns* (5th ed.). Thousand Oaks, CA: Corwin.

Chapter 8

Jensen, E. P. (2009). *Teaching with poverty in mind.* Alexandria, VA: ASCD Books.

Sousa, D. (2005). *How the brain learns* (5th ed.). Thousand Oaks, CA: Corwin.

Chapter 9

Eagleman, D. (2015). *The Brain: The story of you.* New York, NY: Vintage.

Hurst, Aaron. (2014). *The purpose economy: How your desire for impact, personal growth and community is changing the world.* Boise, ID: Elevate.

Chapter 10

Eagleman, D. (2020) *Livewired: The inside story of the ever-changing brain.* New York, NY: Pantheon.

Chapter 11

Bridges, W. (1997) Creating You and Company. DaCapo Press: Cambridge, Massachusetts.

Levinson, J.C. (1984) Guerilla marketing: Secrets for making big profits from your small business. Houghton Mifflin, Boston, Massachusetts.

Chapter 12

Caine, R. N., & Caine, G. (1996). *Making connections: Teaching and the human brain.* Boston, MA: Addison-Wesley Longman, Inc.

Chapter 13

Hanh, T. N. (1987). *The miracle of mindfulness: An introduction to the practice of meditation.* Boston, MA: Beacon Press.

Chapter 15

Feuerstein, R. (1996). *Mediated learning: In and out of the classroom.* Arlington Heights, IL: Skylight.

Chapter 16

Eagleman, D. (2015). *The Brain: The story of you.* New York, NY: Vintage.

Chapter 18

Blanchard, K. *The breakfast of champions.* Retrieved from kenblanchardbooks.com/feedback-is-the-breakfast-of-champions/

Chapter 19

Ambani, N. The Reliance Foundation. reliancefoundation.org

Afterword

Friedman, T. (2017). *Thank you for being late: An optimist's guide to thriving in the age of accelerations.* New York: Farrar, Straus & Giroux.

Key Terms

Bordieu, P. (1977). *Outline of a theory of practice* (Richard Nice, trans.). Cambridge, MA: Cambridge University Press.

Bordieu, P. (1986). The forms of capital. In J. G. Richardson (Ed.), *Handbook of theory and research for the sociology of education* (pp. 241-258). New York, NY: Greenwood.

Coleman, J. (1988). Social capital in the creation of human capital. *American Journal of Sociology*, 94, 95-120.

Cook-Cottone, C. (2004). Constructivism in family literacy practices: Parents as mentors. *Reading Improvement*, 41(4), 208-216.

Feuerstein, R., Feuerstein, R. S., & Falik, L. H. (2010). *Beyond smarter: Mediated learning and the brain's capacity for change.* New York, NY: Teachers College Press.

Fitts, S., & McClure, G. (2015). Building social capital in Hightown: The role of confianza in Latina immigrants' social networks in the new south. *Anthropology and Education Quarterly*, 46(3), 295-311. doi:10.1111/aeq.12108

Hurst, A. (2014). *The purpose economy.* Boise, Idaho: Elevate, A Russell media Company.

Merriam-Webster Dictionary. (2014).

Olivares, R. A. (2002). Communication, constructivism and transfer of knowledge in the education of bilingual learners. *International Journal of Bilingual Education and Bilingualism*, 5(1), 4-19.

Vygotsky, L. S. (1978). *Mind in society: The development of higher psychological processes.* Cambridge, MA: Harvard University Press.

About the Author
Susan F. Tierno, Ed.D.

Dr. Tierno's education career has spanned from K-12 to higher education. Her 501c3 educational foundation, Let's Think-kids Foundation, Inc., channeled her social entrepreneurship by creating school partnerships with teachers, students, and their families with specific training in the **brain** and how to think and learn.

She is a recipient of the National Creative Thinking Recognition Award for innovative programs for teachers, parents, and children from the Creative Thinking Association of America.

Dr. Tierno holds an Ed.D. with a dissertation focused on Hispanic **parent engagement**, which has now evolved into *¡Andamio!: Engaging Hispanic Families for ELL Success Using* **Brain-Based** *Learning,* published by Andamio Press LLC. Her life experiences—and growing up within a military family that descended from immigrants—formed her thinking and shaped her career of service to parents, students, and her fellow teachers.

As a member of the Baby-Boomer generation born in Fort Benning, Georgia, Dr. Tierno is the only daughter in five generations of an Italian family from Abbruzzi, Italy. Because her father was in the military, her life as an "army brat" was rich with travel from Army post to Army post, and she grew up in various parts of the United States and South America.

Her father, who recently passed and was interred at West Point, was a survivor of Pearl Harbor. Her grandmother was a survivor of the Triangle Shirtwaist Factory Fire.

Dr. Tierno attended Marymount College in New York, and spent a month studying in France because that was her selected second language for many years. Shortly thereafter, her father was stationed as the Military Group Commander of Southern Command in La Paz, Bolivia. To prepare for such an educational challenge, she turned her focus to studies in Latin American history, sociology and anthropology.

She requested permission from the dean to conduct an independent study in Bolivia. As a result, for six months she worked with a Resurrection Catholic nun and priest in a small Aymara Indian school, taking several daily bus rides up the mountain to the village school.

She developed a progressive literacy program working with the children there, building stakeholders in the Catholic and military **communities**.

This experience laid the profound groundwork for her already well-familiar passion for teaching, and it added the bilingual perspective that built her background sociologically and anthropologically with cultures of the Third World.

Many years later, Dr. Tierno was not only teaching in bilingual classrooms, but received a master's degree in bilingual education from the University of Texas-Pan American.

Her experience in Bolivia was the beginning of a deep understanding of her personal passion for teaching and its relationship to immigrants and their impact on education today.

Dr. Tierno's life experiences not only led her to teaching in elementary classrooms, but also took her to the positions at University of Texas, Pan American; the University of Nevada, Reno; Post University in Connecticut; and to positions in school publishing companies, where she learned the business of building a business.

Thereafter, she designed her first education 501c3 foundation, dedicated solely to school partnerships with bilingual teachers and their professional development, to their bilingual students, and their families with specific training in how to think and learn using the engagement **model** for children, teachers, and parents.

Her children's project-based writing program, now in its second iteration for parents and third edition for ELLs, was focused not just on writing for ELLs but was built around **mediated** learning.

After taking a break from four replication projects, her lifelong experiences culminated in the dedication of the 501c3 foundation, Let's Think-kids Foundation, Inc. (www.LTKF.org), and its vision of critical and creative thinking and learning for English language learners (ELLs). The first project began with her innovative programs in an urban district in Connecticut.

Now once again, adding the author capstone to her distinguished career in education, she currently lives in Texas and has dedicated herself to the growth of her parent programs, her foundation, her new publishing company, and the creation of additional research articles and books.

Bring Think-parents Are Powerful™ to Your Parent Liaisons!

I hope you have enjoyed this book and found it useful and encouraging. While it is by no means complete, I hope the information on these pages will serve as a springboard for your own creativity as you begin to design effective parent training and engagement programs that work within your unique community and circumstances. Whether you are training face-to-face or virtually, these concepts for parent training will work anywhere.

If you would like more information about consulting, training for your district, my Think-parents are Powerful™ program and tools, or booking a speaker, please contact me!

Dr. Susan F. Tierno
sftierno223@verizon.net
www.LTKF.org

www.ingramcontent.com/pod-product-compliance
Lightning Source LLC
Chambersburg PA
CBHW051358290426
44108CB00015B/2060